New edition

Preparing
for the **BMAT**

The official guide to the BioMedical Admissions Test

www.pearsonschoolsandfe.co.uk

✓ Free online support
✓ Useful weblinks
✓ 24 hour online ordering

0845 630 33 33

Heinemann

Part of Pearson

Heinemann is an imprint of Pearson Education Limited, a company incorporated in England and Wales, having its registered office at Edinburgh Gate, Harlow, Essex, CM20 2JE. Registered company number: 872828

www.pearsonschoolsandfecolleges.co.uk

Heinemann is a registered trademark of Pearson Education Limited

Text © UCLES 2005, 2010

www.admissionstests.cambridgeassessment.org.uk

First published 2005
This edition 2010

ARP Impression 98

British Library Cataloguing in Publication Data
A catalogue record for this book is available from the British Library

ISBN 978 0 435046 87 3

Cambridge Assessment editors: Mark Shannon and Sue Fiander
Edited by Nick Sample, Isabel Thomas and Helen Payne
Typeset by Tech-Set Ltd
Original illustrations © Pearson Education 2010
Illustrated by Emily Hunter-Higgins
Cover design by Ben Wakefield, Eye Design
Printed in Great Britain by Ashford Colour Press Ltd.

Acknowledgements
Page 26: paragraph adapted from Wrangham, R., Jones, J., Laden, G. et al. (1999), The raw and the stolen: cooking and the ecology of human origins, Current Anthropology, Vol. 40, No. 5, pp 567–94 © 1999 by the Wenner-Gren Foundation for Anthropological Research, reproduced with permission of the University of Chicago Press; page 28: paragraph adapted from Hollman, M. (2004), The lingering lessons of Exxon Valdez, Ecologist, Vol. 34, No. 4, p.12; page 38: paragraph adapted from Bell, A. (2003), Employment Law in a Nutshell, Sweet and Maxwell, p.69; page 46: first paragraph and charts © The Economist Newspaper Limited, London (5 April 2003); page 55: paragraphs © Malleson, A. (2002) Whiplash and Other Useful Illnesses, McGill Queens University Press, Montreal, p.254; page 52: Crown Copyright material is reproduced with the permission of the Controller of HMSO and the Queen's Printer for Scotland; page76: graph from Sawka M, Pandolf K (1990), Effects of Body Water Loss on Physiological Function and Exercise Performance, in Gisolfi CV, Lamb DR, Perspectives in Exercise Science & Sports Medicine, Volume 3, Fluid Homeostasis During Exercise, reproduced with permission of Cooper Publishing Group, 251 Knollwood Drive, Traverse City, MI 49686, USA.

Every effort has been made to contact copyright holders of material reproduced in this book. Any omissions will be rectified in subsequent printings if notice is given to the publishers.

Contents

Introduction to the BMAT

This book will provide you with all the information and materials you need to prepare for the BioMedical Admissions Test (BMAT). By giving you the chance to familiarise yourself with the nature of the test, and clear guidance about how your responses will be scored, we aim to give you every opportunity to demonstrate that you have the knowledge and skills needed to cope with the rigours of biomedical study at the highest level.

History of the BMAT

The BMAT was developed within the Research and Evaluation Division of the University of Cambridge Local Examinations Syndicate (now called Cambridge Assessment) and was first administered in November 2003. The BMAT adopted elements of its predecessors, the Cambridge Medical and Veterinary Admissions Test (MVAT) and the Oxford Medicine Admissions Test (OMAT). Each stage in the development of the test was carried out in close consultation with those responsible for teaching preclinical medicine and veterinary medicine at the institutions that use the test.

The BMAT was introduced because these institutions receive many more applications from extremely well qualified students than there are places to offer. The purpose of the test is purely to provide a predictive assessment of candidates' academic potential. No attempt is made to assess fitness to practice medicine, which institutions may do in other ways. The use of BMAT scores in the admissions process varies from institution to institution. For information about how your BMAT scores will be used, you should check the website of the institution to which you have applied or contact the appropriate admissions office.

Structure of the BMAT

The BMAT has three sections:

Section 1 – Aptitude and Skills: 1 hour
35 multiple choice or short answer questions

This section tests the generic skills of Problem Solving, Understanding Argument and Data Analysis and Inference. It is designed to give institutions an insight into your problem solving ability and critical thinking skills. You can't 'cram' for this section, but you will benefit from familiarising yourself with the types of questions that are used, and from developing these skills, which will be useful in future studies.

Section 2 – Scientific Knowledge and Applications: 30 minutes
27 multiple choice or short answer questions

This section tests your ability to apply core scientific and mathematical knowledge and principles (typically covered by the age of 16 in non-specialist school science and mathematics courses). The material covered in this section should be familiar to you, although you may want to check for gaps in your knowledge, especially if you are a mature student or if you were educated outside the UK.

Section 3 – Writing Task: 30 minutes
one question must be answered from a choice of four

This section tests whether you can demonstrate the capacity to develop ideas and communicate them effectively in writing. You will typically be given a choice of four short questions, based on topics of general, medical, scientific or veterinary interest. Your response is restricted to one side of an A4 answer sheet, giving you time to plan your response carefully before you start writing.

How the BMAT is scored

Responses to each section are recorded on separate answer sheets, examples of which are included at the back of this book. Marks on Sections 1 and 2 are converted to scores on the BMAT scale. This runs from 1 (low) to 9 (high), with scores being reported to one decimal place. The scale has been designed so that typical applicants to the most highly selective undergraduate university courses in the UK (who are by definition academically very able) will score around 5.0. The best applicants will score more highly, but 6.0 represents a comparatively high score and only a few very exceptional applicants will achieve BMAT scores higher than 7.0.

Section 3 responses are given a mark for quality of content on a scale from 0 (low) to 5 (high) and a mark for quality of written English on a scale of E (low) to A (high). Each essay is marked twice and the scores given are combined to give a final mark. If the two examiners disagree significantly, the response is marked by a third examiner. Marks will be reported as a number (quality of content) followed by a letter (quality of written English), for example 5A. A more detailed description of the essay scoring process is given in Section 3 of this book.

Scores on each section of the test are reported separately to the institution(s) to which you have applied, together with a scanned image of your essay. The use of BMAT scores in the admissions process varies from institution to institution. For more information about how your scores will be used, you should consult the prospectus or website of the institution(s) to which you have applied, or contact the appropriate admissions office.

Hints and tips

Throughout this book, the authors give advice about how you might approach questions, and what the markers are looking for. However, there are some general recommendations that you should bear in mind:

- **Read the questions carefully**
  In particular, you should note how you are expected to respond. Some multiple choice questions may ask, for example, 'which two of the following...' so you are required to shade two circles and will not receive a mark if you shade only one. Also, many calculations require answers to be given in specific units and it helps to note this before you start the calculation.

- **Write clearly**
  Responses to Sections 1 and 2 are computer-marked, and checked by experienced staff. However, if the intended response is not clear (for example if you take two attempts at a multiple choice question and fail to thoroughly erase the original response, or if a written character is illegible) you will not

receive a mark. Similarly, although the Writing Task is not marked on the basis of neatness of handwriting, if your response is partly illegible, this will inevitably affect the clarity with which you communicate your ideas. In your haste to complete the test, do not jeopardise your chances of being given credit for correct answers by writing illegibly.

- **Answer all questions in Sections 1 and 2**
  The instructions on the question paper state 'There are no penalties for incorrect responses, only points for correct answers, so you should attempt all questions'. This means that if you don't know the answer, or if you are about to run out of time, you should guess. You can increase your chances of guessing the correct answers by first eliminating any options you think are unlikely to be correct. (It may seem odd that we are telling you to guess the answers to our questions, but we would prefer you to read it here than pay to attend an expensive coaching course to hear the same advice.) You should also note that each section is timed separately, so you must answer all the questions in the time allowed for that section.

- **Don't spend too much time on questions that you find difficult**
  The BMAT is designed so that the majority of students should be able to finish each section in the time allowed. However, there may be questions that you find difficult to answer, or which look as though they will take up too much time. If this is the case, move on to the next question, and return to the problem question later if you have time. The BMAT is likely to challenge even the most able candidate. Don't let a few difficult questions distract you; try to focus on completing the questions that you *can* answer.

- **Don't expect the live test to be too similar to the sample materials**
  This advice is particularly relevant to Section 3. In 2004, a small but significant number of Writing Task responses were barely relevant to the question being answered. In many cases, these responses contained material more appropriate to the specimen questions on the BMAT website. The purpose of the Writing Task is to assess your ability to *develop and communicate your ideas effectively in writing*. Responses that are of little relevance to the question, however well written, are unlikely to be rewarded high marks.

Some of these recommendations may seem obvious, but every year very able candidates lose marks because of easily avoidable errors and oversights.

How to register for the BMAT

The majority of candidates register for, and take the test, in the school or college at which they study. Mature students, and others with no links to a school or college, can register to take the test at one of the many BMAT Open Centres, located in the UK and internationally. A full list of Open Centres is available on our website (www.admissionstests.cambridgeassessment.org.uk).

Where to go for more information

Although the information given in this book is correct at the time of going to press, the definitive source of up-to-date BMAT information is the website: www.admissionstests.cambridgeassessment.org.uk

If you still have queries, you can contact us by e-mail at: bmatinfo@cambridgeassessment.org.uk

How to use this book

The following pages contain sample questions from each BMAT section. The questions have been selected to cover the full range of skill areas. Each question is accompanied by the correct answer and a discussion of the best ways to approach similar questions. In Sections 1 and 2, questions are shown on the left-hand page and answers on the right-hand page. You should initially cover the answers and try to solve the questions yourself. Following some questions there is a discussion box where the author further examines that style of question. It is best to read this commentary after you have attempted the question and studied the author's solution.

Questions are set out in the style of the BMAT, so you will know what to expect on the day

Sections 1 and 2 are split into question and answer pages

Margin boxes give you key hints and tips

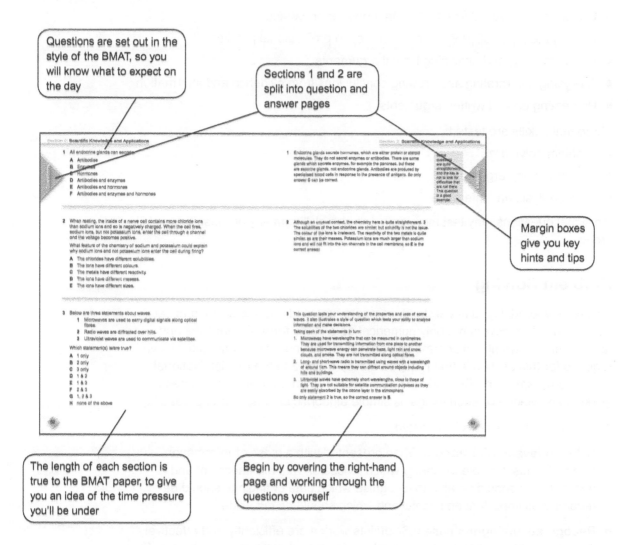

The length of each section is true to the BMAT paper, to give you an idea of the time pressure you'll be under

Begin by covering the right-hand page and working through the questions yourself

Aptitude and Skills

Introduction

Section 1 of the BMAT is designed to test your ability to think, reason and analyse information in a logical manner. The skills tested here are of great value in both undergraduate study and professional employment. They are of particular use in terms of:

- Understanding scientific information, however presented
- Solving the types of problem encountered in professional practice
- Understanding and analysing logical arguments
- Analysing, interpreting and drawing conclusions from evidence and information
- Presenting cogent written arguments

Three main skills are tested:

- Problem solving
- Understanding argument
- Data analysis and inference

Individual questions may test more than one sub-skill from any of these three skill areas.

Problem Solving

This tests your ability to understand, compare, use and analyse mathematical information. This covers not only numerical data in the form of quantities and tables, but also graphs, diagrams and spatial reasoning. The mathematical level required for this section is that required at Key Stage 3 in the English National Curriculum framework. Beyond the basic level of mathematics, this requires a working knowledge of such things as simple algebraic equations and probability.

The following sub-skills will be tested:

- **Select relevant information**: When presented with a mass of information, scientists must be able to identify which pieces of data are important and relevant. You should be able to recognise which data or findings should be regarded as important and useful and which should be put aside.

- **Recognise analogous cases**: Scientists work more efficiently and effectively if they are able to recognise previously encountered patterns in fresh data. By recognising when new information is similar to old information, and in which areas it differs, it is possible to use the new information in more effective ways. This includes the ability to recognise cause and effect in data, and to identify possible reasons for patterns and variations.

- **Determine and apply appropriate procedures**: In order to solve problems, different and sometimes apparently unrelated pieces of data must be combined in appropriate ways. The method of combining the data may not always be obvious and may require an informed search either of the data or of the possible methods of using it.

Different problems require different strategies to solve them. By simply playing with the numbers given, you might be lucky and hit on the right answer, but it is normally preferable to work systematically. Read the entire question before trying to work anything out. The most important thing is to recognise what you are being asked. Some of the information given may not be needed to deduce the solution.

Questions in the category 'Determine and apply appropriate procedures' are at the heart of Problem Solving as they require you to find a method of using the data to produce a solution. There are rarely standard ways of approaching problems like these. It is better to start by approaching the problem from both ends. Ask yourself: What information is needed to produce the answer? How can I calculate this from the data I have?

Sometimes solving the problem will require a search. This may be as simple as finding the required data point from a large mass of information. In other cases, you may need to consider many possible options (for example, which sums cannot be made from a group of coins). In this case, a very systematic process would be required to make sure you do not miss anything. Alternatively, the search may be necessary to find the *method* of solution. In this case it is not so easy to be systematic, but you must ensure that your method is leading to the values you need (possibly as intermediate steps).

The time given for the BMAT test is limited, so you will need to work quickly and effectively. Even so, it is often worth taking a few seconds to check each answer. In many cases this could involve substituting the answer back into the original problem. This is less practical if you have had to do a search – in this case it is better to ensure that the method you used in the first place covered all possibilities.

Understanding Argument

The questions that fall into this category can be grouped under the following sub-skills:

- **Analysis**: Identifying reasons, assumptions and conclusions in short arguments.

- **Evaluation**: Detecting flaws; recognising weaknesses and strengths; assessing responses which challenge or support arguments.

- **Inference**: Drawing reliable conclusions, and recognising unsafe ones.

Much of the reasoning we are presented with in the media is weak or defective. Many of the inferences writers and commentators draw from available information is unsafe. The skills of analysing and assessing argument are therefore of huge importance, especially in situations where the consequences of poor reasoning are potentially very serious.

The Understanding Argument component of the BMAT tests critical thinking skills. These questions require critical understanding and/or appraisal.

Most of the questions are based on a short piece of text with multiple choice answers, though sometimes a single word or numerical answer is required.

Questions are often phrased in one of the following ways:

- Which of the following is the main conclusion of the above argument?
- Which of the following, though not explicitly stated, is an assumption in the above argument?
- Which of the following is a claim which would weaken (or support) the above argument?
- Which of the following identifies/exposes/describes a flaw in the argument?
- Which of the following conclusions can be drawn from the above information?

Not every question will closely match one of these examples. Some questions test a combination of skills, or approach the problem from a different angle; much depends on the nature of the stimulus material. You may be asked to:

- clarify an ambiguous term
- explain an anomaly or discrepancy
- describe the logical function of a word or phrase
- assess a definition, or
- supply a missing piece in a chain of reasoning.

If you have studied some logic you may find it useful as one way to approach a task. But questions that require a knowledge of formal or symbolic logic, or which give any marked advantage to someone with such knowledge, will not come up in the test. For example, you will never be asked to supply the technical *name* of a particular logical fallacy, though you will sometimes be asked to identify what is wrong with certain kinds of argument.

A grasp of some *semi*-technical vocabulary is assumed. This includes terms such as conclusion, reason (or premise), assumption, explanation, inference, implication and consequence. You will be expected to distinguish between necessary and sufficient conditions, general and particular statements, cause and correlation, and to recognise relations such as consistency, contradiction, compatibility and equivalence.

Above all, your preparation for the BMAT should help you to develop the ability to *think around* a question. Many of the stimulus passages will exhibit several different features that concern the critical thinker. On the day of the test you will be asked a relatively specific question on each one. You will be far better prepared if you have acquired the habit of asking yourself a whole range critical questions: What is the conclusion? Does the conclusion follow from the reasons? Is anything assumed beyond what is stated, and if so is it a reasonable assumption? How would *I* challenge or support this argument? If I accept the conclusion, to what else do I commit myself?

You will not have time to think around a stimulus passage in this comprehensive way in the live test. But as you prepare, it is useful to tackle sample questions without giving yourself a time limit. The more effectively you can get to grips with an argument, asking your own questions and anticipating the answers, the more quickly and confidently you will be able to select the correct response on the day.

As you work through the sample questions in this book you will see suggestions for 'thinking around' questions. Try to apply these to every question, and to arguments you come across day-to-day. It will quickly become a natural response – and a very useful one to acquire.

Data Analysis and Inference

The final type of question in Section 1 requires the application of the skills described above to handling and interpreting larger amounts of information. The *stimulus* for these questions may include verbal, tabular, graphical, statistical and/or diagrammatic elements.

When presented with such data, the student or professional must be able to understand the information, select those pieces of data that are relevant to the problem and analyse the writing, author's interpretation, methods of data collection and conclusions in a critical manner.

Each stimulus is followed by four to six questions relating to the information presented. Some of the questions will require you to use the skills described under Problem Solving and Understanding Argument. There will also be questions which test the following skills:

- **Data interpretation**: This requires you to draw additional meaning from the information given, for example by obtaining values derived from the data or by considering possible causes for variation shown in data.

- **Data analysis**: The data given in the question may require further manipulation (for example, taking the means of relevant subsets) in order to highlight structure.

- **Inference and deduction**: You are asked to draw conclusions from the information.

Recording your answers

Answers to Section 1 questions may be requested in a variety of forms:

1 A numerical or short verbal answer

2 Single multiple choice (select one from four or five possible answers)

3 Multiple answers (select all possible answers from three or four choices)

See page 99 for a sample response sheet.

The purpose of aptitude and skills testing is to evaluate your ability to think in a certain way. For this reason the paper will always contain questions that cannot be solved using formulaic or learned methods. Such questions should be approached flexibly. There is a limited amount of information in each question and therefore a finite number of ways in which the information can be combined. Sometimes an intermediate result must be discovered before you can proceed to the final solution. There is not necessarily a 'right' way to solve these questions. You should be prepared to try different ways of using the data to find an effective route to the solution.

The time for the test is limited, so the possible solution methods must be scanned efficiently and quickly. Marks can be maximised by answering every question – even if it is necessary to guess. Questions vary in difficulty, so it is often better to leave a harder question (or one that you are having trouble with) until the end.

Skill: Problem Solving

Sub-skill: Select Relevant Information

1 The figures below show the results of a survey of 1000 people on the sizes of their current and previous car:

		Current car			
		Large	Medium	Small	Total
Previous car	Large	100	120	20	240
	Medium	80	200	80	360
	Small	40	160	200	400
	Total	220	480	300	1000

If this table is representative of those who are looking to change their car at present, what percentage of purchasers would you expect to trade up to a larger car than their present one?

A 12%

B 22%

C 24%

D 28% ✓

E 70%

N° people who traded up = 40 + 160 + 80.

= 280

$\frac{280}{1000} \times 100$

= 28%

1   You need to recognise which parts of the table are relevant to the question, and how to use these values to arrive at the correct answer. The data relates to people's last change of car, but the question is about people's intentions on buying their next car. At face value these may seem to be two different things. However, we are told that the table is representative of those who are looking to change their car at present. This means that we could equally rewrite the table headings so that 'Current car' is on the left and 'Next car' is on the top.

It is important to read all the information carefully.

Having understood the information given, be clear about what the question wants you to find – the percentage of purchasers likely to trade up to a larger car than their present model. One such group is those whose current car is medium and previous car was small. We can list all the groups which fit the requirement of the question:

Current car	Previous car	Number
Large	Medium	80
Large	Small	40
Medium	Small	160

When doing the question at speed, mark relevant groups directly onto the table in the question.

On the basis of this survey, you would expect 280 people to trade up. The final step is to calculate the appropriate percentage correctly. The total number surveyed was 1000, so:

$$\frac{280}{1000} \times 100 = 28\%$$

The correct answer is **D**. The fact that this is one of the choices given may improve our confidence that it is correct, but we must be wary as the question setters choose the alternative options to represent easily made mistakes.

If time allows, double-check your working.

2 Twelve teams will take part in the Pitchball World Cup next month. They will compete in two pools of six. Every team will play two matches against each of the other teams in the same pool and one match against each team in the other pool. The winners of each pool will then contest the final.

How many matches will be played altogether during the tournament?

A 67

B 91

C 97 ✓

D 109

E 193

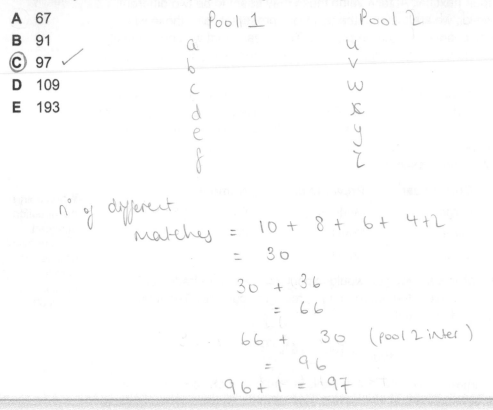

Pool 1   Pool 2

a   u
b   v
c   w
d   x
e   y
f   z

n° of different
matches = 10 + 8 + 6 + 4 + 2
       = 30

30 + 36
   = 66

66 + 30 (pool 2 inter)
   = 96

96 + 1 = 197

3 A survey of methods of transport to school has been carried out. The results, broken down by year group, are shown below.

	Year 7	Year 8	Year 9	Year 10	Year 11	Total
Car	30	33	16	18	10	102
Bus	14	16	13	15	18	76
Bicycle	5	12	23	25	30	95
Walk	101	89	100	92	108	490
Total	150	145	152	150	166	763

One of the individual entries in the above table has been typed incorrectly, although the marginal totals are correct. Which value is wrong?

A 14

B 33 ✓

C 23

D 92

E 18

2   This question requires care in reading the rules of the tournament and using a systematic recording system to ensure that all matches are counted. Never take anything for granted.

The tournament takes part in three phases.

Phase 1: Every team will play two matches against each of the other teams in the same pool. There are six teams. Team A must play teams B, C, D, E and F twice – 10 matches. Additionally team B must play teams C, D, E and F twice (you have already counted the matches against team A) – 8 matches. Similarly, team C plays an extra 6, team D an extra 4 and team E an extra 2. This makes a total of $10 + 8 + 6 + 4 + 2 = 30$ in the first pool and a similar 30 in the second pool – 60 games in total in phase 1.

Phase 2: Every team plays one match against each of the teams in the other pool. If we call the teams in the other pool P, Q, R, S, T and U, then A must play all of them and so must B, C, D, E and F. Each has 6 games, making 36 in total. Note that this time you only need to count each match once; you have counted B vs R so you do not need to count R vs B as a separate match. There is no need to double the answer for the two pools either, as you have already counted for both.

Phase 3: The winners of each pool will then contest the final. Phase 3 consists of a single match.

The total is: $60 + 36 + 1 = 97$ matches. Option **C** is correct.

It is not sufficient, having obtained an answer on the multiple choice list, to be confident that it is correct. For example, if we had only counted one pool in phase 1, we would have obtained: $30 + 36 + 1 = 67$ matches. This is option **A**. Remember that the incorrect options are chosen as apparently plausible answers that could be obtained through an error in the logic or calculation.

> Break the information down into pieces that can be analysed separately.

> Use numbers or letters instead of names to save time. information.

3   The most straightforward and systematic method of finding the incorrect value is to sum all the rows and columns and identify which two are wrong. The desired value will be at the intersection. If you do this, you will find that the Year 8 column adds to 150 (not 145) and the Car row adds to 107 (not 102). These intersect at the value 33, so **B** is the correct answer.

Luckily, you only had to sum two columns and one row before finding the error. If you really wanted to be sure, you could continue to check the remaining row and column totals.

Under time pressure, there is a much faster way to solve this problem. It contains a slight risk, but the potential time saved means that it is worth trying in the first instance. If we just sum the units place of each number, we can very rapidly check whether the error is in a particular row or column. For example, in the Year 7 column $0 + 4 + 5 + 1 = 10$, so 0 is correct as the units value of the column total. We rapidly find that in the next column $3 + 6 + 2 + 9$ adds to something ending in 0, not 5. This saves a lot of addition and reduces the room for error. It will only work if the error is in the units – if the error was 42 instead of 32 this method would not give a result. However, it only takes a few seconds and, if it fails, you can return to the full additions.

> The keys to answering questions in this section are careful reading of the question and systematic working.

> You need to find a balance between double-checking answers and completing as many questions as possible.

Skill: Problem Solving

Sub-skill: Recognise Analogous Cases

4   Which **two** of these statements are equivalent?

   (A) Anne is not older than Susan. $a \leq s$

   B   Susan is younger than Anne. $s < a$

   (C) Susan is at least as old as Anne. $s \geqslant a$

   D   Anne is not younger than Susan. $a \geqslant s$

4 At first glance, this seems easy – there is very little information to absorb. However, the language of each statement is quite different. Most candidates will have to translate the information into a different form before the answer becomes obvious.

There are often several different ways to solve a problem.

Here are three possible ways of approaching the problem.

1. Express each statement as a mathematical inequality. If a represents Anne's age and s represents Susan's age, the statements may be rewritten as follows:

    A $a \leqslant s$ **B** $s < a$ **C** $s \geqslant a$ **D** $a \geqslant s$

    As inequalities may be reversed ($a < s$ is equivalent to $s > a$), you can immediately see that statements **A** and **C** are equivalent.

2. Change the wording of each statement so they are all in similar forms, for example using 'older' in all statements to remove any confusion between comparisons:

    A Anne is not older than Susan. (unchanged)

    B Anne is older than Susan.

    C Susan is at least as old as Anne.

    D Anne is at least as old as Susan.

    If we now turn statement **C** round (so Anne is first), **C** becomes identical to **A**.

3. Summarise the information in a table. This is probably the easiest method to understand and the most reliable if you are not familiar with mathematical or verbal logic.

    There are only three possibilities: Anne is older than Susan, they are both the same age, or Susan is older than Anne. This information can be expressed in a table.

	Anne is older than Susan	Anne and Susan are the same age	Anne is younger than Susan
A Anne is not older than Susan.	NO	YES	YES
B Susan is younger than Anne.	YES	NO	NO
C Susan is at least as old as Anne.	NO	YES	YES
D Anne is not younger than Susan.	YES	YES	NO

Expressing the data visually reduces the different types of information to a simple form.

You can immediately see that statements **A** and **C** are equivalent.

5 The display of a digital clock is made up of 15 coloured lights. The numbers 0 to 9 may be shown on this display as follows.

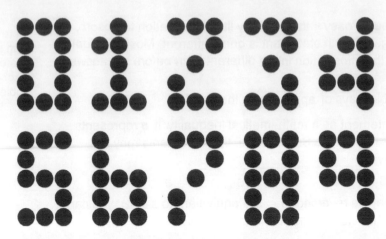

If one of the lights fails, which two numbers might appear identical?

0 and 8 ✓

5 This is an example of a spatial reasoning question. In this case the objects are 2D and you are looking for differences. In other cases you will be asked to recognise the effect of a rotation or reflection. In some questions the objects are 3D and you may need to infer what they look like when viewed from other directions.

A systematic way to approach this question is by using paired comparisons. If you look at two numbers at a time, it is quite easy to see whether a single light would cause confusion between the two. Working systematically, comparisons are made between 0 and 1, 0 and 2, 0 and 3 and so on.

You will quickly find that the correct answer is 0 and 8. If the central light failed, 8 would become identical to 0. However, if the correct answer had been 8 and 9, it would have required 45 comparisons to solve the problem.

Another method is to look at each number in turn and visualise what it would look like with one of the lights out. This can be done quickly for each number, but the correct answer is not found until you reach 8. You may find it quicker to simply scan all the numbers and focus on those with similar shapes. Most of the numbers will be instantly rejected and a more careful comparison carried out for only a few pairs, such as 2 and 3.

Practice will help you to choose the best strategy for questions that require a search.

6 The volume of a solid with a uniform cross section and equivalent points top and bottom joined by straight lines (e.g. a cube or a cylinder or the solid shown as 1 below) is equal to the base area multiplied by the height.

The volume of a solid which has a flat base joint by straight lines to a point at the top (e.g. a cone or a square pyramid or the solid shown as 2 below) is equal to $\frac{1}{3}$ of the base area multiplied by the height.

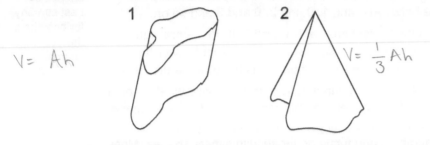

1

$V = Ah$

2

$V = \frac{1}{3}Ah$

For which of the following solids is the volume equal to half the base area multiplied by the height?

$2 \quad V = \frac{1}{2}Ah$

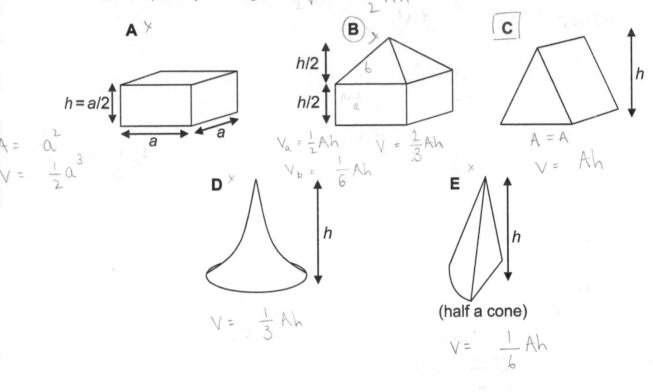

A

$h = a/2$

$a \qquad a$

$A = a^2$

$V = \frac{1}{2}a^3$

B

$h/2$

$h/2$

6

$A = A$

a

$V_a = \frac{1}{2}Ah \qquad V = \frac{2}{3}Ah$

$V_b = \frac{1}{6}Ah$

C

h

$A = A$

$V = Ah$

D

h

$V = \frac{1}{3}Ah$

E

h

(half a cone)

$V = \frac{1}{6}Ah$

6 There are many ways to approach this question. The first step is to understand the information given and what is required. Two rules are given which describe the volume of certain classes of solid. You are asked to identify which solid can be described by a third rule, i.e. falls in between the other two classes of solid.

The most systematic way to proceed is to see whether you can calculate the volume of each solid shown using the two rules you have been given.

Solid **A** conforms to rule 1. The top and bottom are identical and joined by straight lines. Its volume will be equal to the base area multiplied by the height.

Solid **B** does not fit either of the rules. However, it may be divided into two solids – a cuboid and a pyramid – and the volume of each calculated using the rules we are given. If A is the base area:

$$\text{Volume of cuboid} = A \times \frac{h}{2} \quad \text{and Volume of pyramid} = A \times \frac{h}{2} \times \frac{1}{3} = A \times \frac{h}{6}$$

$$\text{So total volume} = A \times \left(\frac{h}{2} + \frac{h}{6}\right) = A \times \frac{2h}{3}$$

The volume of this solid is $\frac{2}{3} \times$ base area $\times$ height, so it is not the one we are looking for.

There is a quicker way to eliminate **B**. If we just look at the bottom cuboid, it will clearly have half the volume of a cuboid with twice the height (i.e. one with height the same as the solid shown in **B**). Since this is $\frac{1}{2} \times$ base area $\times$ total height $= \frac{1}{2} \times A \times h$, the addition of the pyramid at the top must make it more than the volume we are looking for.

Solid **C** does not conform to either of the rules and a method to estimate its volume using only the information given is not immediately obvious. The best thing to do is to put this one aside until you have looked at the rest.

Solid **D** is not a cone, but if we imagine a cone with the same base, it will have a larger volume than the solid shown in **D**. This means that **D** must have a volume less than $\frac{1}{3} \times$ base area $\times$ height and is not the one we are looking for.

Solid **E** conforms to rule 2. It has a flat base joined by straight lines to a point at the top. Its volume is, therefore, $\frac{1}{3} \times$ base area $\times$ height.

By elimination, you can conclude that solid **C** is the only one that could possibly have a volume calculated by $\frac{1}{2} \times$ base area $\times$ height.

This is a perfectly valid method of solving the problem. However, if you have time you can increase your confidence in your answer by performing a simple check. There is a simple method of doing this, which requires only a little ability at spatial reasoning.

Imagine two solids identical to **C**, stacked together as shown:

We now have a solid which conforms to rule 1 – its volume is base area $\times$ height. Therefore a single solid **C** must have a volume equal to half of this, or $\frac{1}{2} \times$ base area $\times$ height.

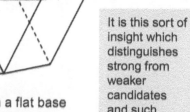

A confident candidate might be able to infer that, if a solid with a flat base and top has a volume of base area $\times$ height, and if another solid with flat base and pointed top has a volume of $\frac{1}{3} \times$ base area $\times$ height, then a third solid with a flat base and linear top must have an area in between the two.

This solution may seem long winded but, as with many of these problems, the astute candidate will be able to perform most of the steps very quickly.

It is this sort of insight which distinguishes strong from weaker candidates and such skills can be developed by practice.

Skill: Problem Solving

Sub-skill: Determine and apply appropriate procedures

7   A cheetah's top speed is 110 km/h and that of a zebra is 60 km/h. If both are running at top speed in a straight line and the cheetah is 100 m behind, how many seconds will it take the cheetah to catch the zebra?

$110 - 60$

$= 50 \text{ km/h}$

$S = \dfrac{d}{t}$

$t = \dfrac{d}{S} =$

$t = \dfrac{0 \cdot 1}{50} \times 3600$

$= \dfrac{36}{5} = 7 \cdot 2 s$ ✓

8   Three friends decide to weigh themselves on a public weighing machine using only one coin. They are not thinking clearly and do not realise that they could measure their individual weights directly. First John and Ivan get on and the machine shows 90 kg. Ivan gets off and Kevin gets on – the machine shows 95 kg. Finally John gets off and Ivan gets back on, the machine then shows 99 kg.

They are now left with the problem of working out their individual weights. How much does John weigh?

$J + I = 90$

$J + k = 95$

$I + k = 99$

$I = 99 - k$

$k = 95 - J$

$I = 99 - 95 + J$

$= 4 + J$

$J + J + 4 = 90$

$2J = 86$

$J = 43 \text{ kg}$ ✓

7 Questions vary in complexity and difficulty. This one has relatively few pieces of information (just three numbers) and is quite straightforward to solve.

The actual speeds are not important in this case; the relative speed of the two animals is the focus. The cheetah runs 50 km/h faster than the zebra. We can now consider the situation as being exactly the same as if the zebra was standing still and the cheetah was 100 m away and approaching at 50 km/h.

The calculation is now quite simple: the time taken is $\dfrac{\text{distance}}{\text{speed}}$.

You must use consistent units to calculate the answer – in this case start with km, h and km/h.

The cheetah is 100 m or 0.1 km away so:

$$\text{time} = \frac{0.1}{50}\,\text{h}$$

You are asked for the answer in seconds. There are 3600 seconds in one hour, so:

$$\text{time} = 3600 \times \frac{0.1}{50} = 7.2 \text{ seconds}$$

If you have difficulty remembering the relationship between time, distance and speed, remember that speed is expressed as a distance divided by a time e.g. km/h. All related formulae can be calculated from this.

A significant proportion of questions use speed, distance and time in various ways. This is another area where familiarity through practice will help.

8 You might recognise this as a problem in linear equations: three equations in three unknowns. These may be written as follows:

$$j+i = 90$$
$$j+k = 95$$
$$i+k = 99$$

(j, i, k are respectively John, Ivan and Kevin's weights).

If we add the first two together we have:

$$2j+i+k = 185$$

Subtracting the third:

$$2j = 86$$

So j, John's weight, is 43 kg.

Although many candidates will be familiar with situations involving two simultaneous equations, it may not be as clear how to solve three equations.

There is an equally simple way to tackle this problem for those with less confidence in formal mathematical techniques. If we add the results of each weighing together ($90 + 95 + 99 = 284$ kg), we know everybody has been weighed twice, so their total weight must be 142 kg. We can then find John's weight by subtracting Ivan and Kevin's combined weights: $142 - 99 = 43$ kg.

An intuitive approach to problems can lead to rapid and effective solutions.

9 In a trial of a drug intended to relieve depression, 15% of those tested claimed it made them feel worse, 20% said it produced a slight improvement and 35% said it led to a significant improvement. Of the remaining people in the sample, 9 said it had no effect and the other 27 failed to complete the course of treatment.

How many people initially participated in the trial?

A   36

B   66

C   90

D   106

E   120

(handwritten: 36 = 30%)

(handwritten: 120)

10 Rajesh and Leena are brother and sister and go to the same school which is 2 km from their home. Leena leaves each morning 10 minutes before Rajesh and walks. Rajesh cycles to school by the same route at four times Leena's walking speed and arrives there 5 minutes before her.

How far from home is Leena when Rajesh leaves?

A $\frac{1}{2}$ km

B $\frac{2}{3}$ km

C   1 km

D $1\frac{1}{3}$ km

E $1\frac{1}{2}$ km

(handwritten work:)

L
T
S
d = 2

R
T − 15
4S
d = 2

$S = \dfrac{d}{t}$

$TS = (T − 15)\,4S$

$TS = 4TS − 60S$

$60S = 3TS$

$T = 20\ mins$

$S = \dfrac{2\,km}{20\,min}$

$= 1\,km/10\,min$

9   This question contains a lot of numbers. You must find a suitable way of using them together in order to solve the problem. You are asked to find the number of people in the trial – this means you have to calculate the actual number associated with the percentages.

We are given three percentages (with no overlap between the classes). These add up to 70%, leaving 30% unaccounted for. We are told that this remainder consists of 9 with no effect and 27 who did not complete the trial, 36 in total.

These 36 must represent the 30% who were originally unaccounted for. We now have a number and a corresponding percentage. So the number starting the trial was:

$$\frac{100}{30} \times 36 = 120$$

E is the correct answer.

> This two-directional approach can be useful in this type of problem. Others require a search or an intuitive leap.

10   In order to find out how far Leena is from home when Rajesh leaves, i.e. the distance she walks in 10 minutes, you need to calculate her walking speed.

You know that Leena takes four times as long to get to school and that the difference between their journey times is 15 minutes. Three times as long as Rajesh's journey must be 15 minutes, so his journey takes 5 minutes and Leena's takes 20 minutes.

Using the relationship speed $= \dfrac{\text{distance}}{\text{time}}$, you can calculate that Rajesh travels at 24 km/h and Leena at 6 km/h (these figures tie in with the relative speeds given in the question).

Leena leaves 10 minutes before Rajesh. In 10 minutes ($\frac{1}{6}$ hr) she has walked $6 \times \frac{1}{6} = 1$ km. **C** is the correct answer.

If you are comfortable with algebraic methods, this can be solved more directly. If we call Leena's walking speed s km/h, then Rajesh's cycling speed is $4s$ km/h. The distance to school is 2 km, so Leena takes $2/s$ hours and Rajesh takes $\frac{2}{4}s$ hours. The difference between these times is 15 minutes ($\frac{1}{4}$ hr) so:

$$\frac{2}{s} - \frac{2}{4s} = \frac{1}{4}$$

Multiplying both sides of the equation by $4s$ gives:

$$8 - 2 = s,$$

so s, Leena's walking speed, is 6 km/h. The problem can then be completed as above.

> This problem may be approached using the two-directional method.

> As you produce new values, double-check them against the original information.

> Many problem solving questions can be solved using either formal mathematics or logical reasoning. Use the method that suits you best.

11 Katy, Louise, Mike and Neil all attend regular fitness clinics.

At the beginning of the year, they weighed 65, 80, 75 and 70 kg respectively. During the year, all had a change in weight of more than 5 kg. Mike lost more weight than either Louise or Katy. Neil put on weight.

Which **one** of the following is **not** a possible increasing order of their weights at the end of the year?

A Katy, Louise, Mike, Neil

B Mike, Katy, Louise, Neil

C Mike, Louise, Katy, Neil

D Katy, Mike, Louise, Neil

K   L   M   N
65   80   75   70
60   75   70   75

11 You could approach this by two-way comparisons, but this is potentially a very time consuming procedure. For example Katy started at 65 kg and Mike at 75 kg. Mike lost more than Katy and both lost more than 5 kg. This means that at the end of the year, they could be in either order, so we cannot distinguish between the four options using only this pair – we must try others.

We know that Neil put on weight, so at the end of the year he could not be lighter than Katy who was lighter and lost weight. But this doesn't help as Katy and Neil are in the same order in each option.

We know that Mike lost more weight than either Louise or Katy. We have already compared Katy and Mike. However, Mike started lighter than Louise and lost more weight, so he could not have finished heavier than Louise. This means that option **A** is the one that cannot be possible.

You can save time by looking carefully at the orders in the four options. All have Neil as the heaviest, so comparing Neil with anybody cannot possibly distinguish between them. Reducing the work to three people means the number of two-way comparisons drops from 6 to 3.

Summarising the information in a line diagram makes it easier to see what effect the possible changes may have.

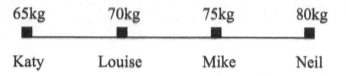

65kg	70kg	75kg	80kg
Katy	Louise	Mike	Neil

Such a diagram can be drawn very quickly and gives considerable help in solving the problem.

A quicker way to approach this question is with logical thought. Mike started the year lighter than Louise and lost more weight, so he could not be heavier than Louise at the end. This gives option **A** as the incorrect one immediately.

A simple diagram can often help you think about a problem more clearly.

12 Of the 100 screws in my work box:

> 60 are cross-headed and 40 are slot-headed
>
> 70 are 3 mm diameter, 20 are 4 mm diameter and 10 are 5 mm diameter
>
> 80 are 50 mm long, 5 are 35 mm long and 15 are 20 mm long.

What is the smallest number of cross-headed, 3 mm diameter, 50 mm long screws that there could be in the box?

A 0

B 10

C 30

D 31

E 60

12 We have seen questions with a range of difficulties. This one is quite hard. Like most of the other questions in this category, there are various ways to approach it.

The direct approach is to use the information in the order it is given. The first piece of information is that there are 100 screws in total. Of these 60 are cross-headed, reducing the maximum in the category at which we are looking to 60.

70 of the 100 screws are 3 mm long. The worst case scenario is that the 30 screws that are *not* 3 mm long are all cross-headed. This would leave only 30 cross-headed, 3 mm screws.

Finally, we know that there are 80 (out of the 100) 50 mm screws. In the worst case, the 20 that are *not* 50 mm long could all be cross-headed and 3 mm in diameter. This leaves 10 as the minimum possible number of cross-headed, 3 mm diameter, 50 mm screws. **B** is the correct answer.

In this case a simple diagram can be used to illustrate the sorting of objects into categories. Looking at the first two sorting criteria:

A table or diagram can be used to put the data into a form in which it can be used more easily.

Cross head (60)		Slot head (40)
4 or 5 mm diameter (30)	3 mm diameter (70)	
	Minimum overlap (30)	

The middle section of this diagram was drawn as shown to arrange the maximum overlap between the desired category on the first criterion (head type) and the non-desired category on the second criterion (diameter). This ensures that the marked region is the minimum overlap which the question required. We can then repeat the process using the 30 desired screws in the first two categories and the 80 desired screws in the final category:

Cross head 3 mm diameter min (30)	Slot head or 4 or 5 mm diameter (70)
25 or 20 mm long (20)	50 mm long (80)
	Minimum overlap (10)

This gives a minimum of 10, as before.

13 Two lighthouses can be seen from the sea-front at Shoreton. Both lights switch on and off in regular repeating patterns. One is on for 3 seconds then off for 8 seconds, whilst the other is on for 2 seconds then off for 7 seconds.

15 seconds ago both lights became visible at precisely the same moment.

In how many seconds from now will both lights next disappear from view together?

A 32

B 47

C 62

D 84

E 131

① 3 , 14 , 25 , 36 , 4<u>7</u> , 58 , 69

② 2 , 11 , 20 , 29 , 38 , 4<u>7</u>

47 - 15
= 32

The nature of the problem would have been completely different if the sequences had been much longer. For example, if lighthouse 1 was on for 7 seconds and off for 16, and lighthouse 2 was on for 8 seconds and off for 23. As an extra activity, consider alternative ways of approaching this problem.

(The answer is that they go off together 583 seconds after they start together. This would be very tedious to diagram or list, so a mathematical approach is necessary.)

13 At first glance, this seems like a simple mathematical problem, which it would be if we were asked when the lights next *appear* together. However, asking when the lights will *disappear* together turns this into a problem solving question. No method for finding the solution is immediately obvious, so part of the problem is to find a method and apply it.

Two methods present themselves as being reliable (although possibly time-consuming). Firstly, you could draw a diagram. The only problem is that it needs to be reasonably accurate. White represents 'on' and black 'off' each small box represents one second. The diagram starts from when the lights come on together:

Lighthouse 1

Lighthouse 2

Lights go off together

The lights go off together after four complete cycles of the first light plus one 'on' period: $4 \times 11 + 3 = 47$ seconds.

There is an extra twist to this problem. If you read the question carefully, you will see that it says that '15 seconds ago both lights became visible at precisely the same moment'. This means that to get the correct answer we must subtract the 15 from the 47 we just calculated, giving 32 seconds. So **A** is the correct answer.

> Always ensure that you don't overlook a significant piece of information.

An alternative is simply to list the 'off' times for the two lights. Starting from the time when they both go on together, the 'off' times are:

Lighthouse 1: 3, 14, 25, 36, 47, 58, 69, ...

Lighthouse 2: 2, 11, 20, 29, 38, 47, ...

So the first time they go off *together* is 47 seconds as before.

This method was very quick and is clearly the best method of solution for this problem as it stands.

> Although a diagram is often the best way of approaching such problems, in this case the accuracy required makes it difficult in the time available.

Skill: Understanding Argument

14 *Homo erectus* appeared 1.9 million years ago. It was 60% larger than its *Australopithecine* predecessor and had a significantly increased brain size, as well as a smaller, flatter gut, differently angled ribs and smaller teeth and mouth. The trigger for this huge evolutionary change has to be the advent of cooking, despite the scant evidence for human control of fire earlier than 400,000 years ago. Heating breaks down indigestible molecules and makes them digestible. Starch in uncooked roots, for example, is often in crystalline form. Until it's heated, our digestive systems can't use it. That means our ancestors could obtain as much nutrition from one roasted tuber as they could from several raw ones, and therefore needed to eat less. Cooking also softens food, diminishing the need for big teeth that can shear and pulverise. Smaller teeth also mean smaller faces, as well as much smaller mouths.

Which one of the following best expresses the main conclusion of the above argument?

A The appearance of *Homo erectus* brought about huge evolutionary changes in the species.

B By diminishing the need for big powerful teeth, cooking gave our ancestors smaller faces and smaller mouths.

C Cooking must be the explanation for the evolutionary changes that came with the appearance of *Homo erectus.*

D *Homo erectus* needed to eat less than its predecessor, *Australopithecus*, to obtain the same amount of nutrition.

E There is little evidence for human use of fire for cooking until long after the appearance of *Homo erectus*.

14 The specific task here is to identify the conclusion. You need to analyse the argument in order to distinguish between the conclusion and the supporting reasons, together with any contextual information that may be included in the passage.

The text is a scientific argument, which is a useful clue as to its structure. Typically the conclusion of a scientific argument is a *hypothesis*, which is supported by evidence. This passage is no exception: it starts out by noting certain facts, i.e. the evolutionary changes that evidently coincided with the emergence of *Homo erectus*. Then it advances a hypothesis about the cause (or causal explanation) for those facts – namely that cooking must have been the 'trigger'.

Here, in an abbreviated form, is an analysis of the argument.

Context (facts to be explained)

Homo erectus appeared 1.9 million years ago. 60% larger than predecessor; significantly increased brain size; smaller teeth and mouth… etc.

Reasoning (evidence given in support of the conclusion)

1. Heating makes food more digestible, so there is the same nutrition from less food
2. Cooking softens food, therefore less need for big teeth
3. If smaller teeth, then smaller faces/mouths

Conclusion

The trigger for this huge evolutionary change has to be the advent of cooking.

The correct response is therefore **C**.

Inserting the word 'therefore' or 'so' between claims you have selected as reasons and the one you have chosen as the conclusion is a useful check: if it doesn't make sense, then you almost certainly need to think again.

Alternatively you can rearrange the claims and link them with 'because':

The trigger must have been cooking

because

1. Heating makes food digestible; 2. Cooking softens food…etc.

All that remains is to check that none of the other options is viable as the conclusion. **A** is the general fact that the passage is seeking to explain, so it is not the conclusion. **B** and **D** are each reasons offered for the conclusion. **E** is an observation which follows the conclusion, in parentheses, but if anything *counters* the conclusion. It acknowledges that there is not much evidence that humans were using fire for cooking (which would explain why it has previously been rejected as a sound hypothesis). In effect the author is arguing that cooking explains the changes *despite* what **E** says, because the other, circumstantial evidence is sufficiently strong. You may not agree with the claim, but it is the conclusion nonetheless.

The kind of detailed analysis we have looked at here is obviously too time-consuming to carry out in the test, where you will only have a couple of minutes to answer each question. But if you practise it carefully and methodically during preparation for the test it will be time well spent.

Being able to sort and label the various claims in a text is probably the most reliable way of identifying the conclusion, and of satisfying yourself that you have grasped the logical structure of the argument.

You will soon acquire a 'feel' for common patterns of argument which will allow you to recognise the constituent parts quickly and confidently. Develop your own analysis techniques and practise them on different arguments until it becomes second nature. It will not only be useful for questions like this one – identifying conclusions – but for all the questions that test understanding argument.

15 The worst of what ensued when the Exxon Valdez spilled 40,000 tons of crude oil into Alaska's coastal waters in 1989 is not that it was the most damaging oil spill in history but that it isn't yet history. Despite the intense research on the ecosystem, this 10,000-square-mile tapestry of ice fields, mountains, forests and sea is far from recovered. Lingering and unanticipated injuries abound. A 2001 study found more than 100 tons of toxic oil remaining on dozens of the beaches, oil that seeps out with every tide, and that—because incomplete weathering left behind higher concentrations of toxins—is even more poisonous now than when it gushed from the ripped tanker. This oil will remain on these beaches for decades to come.

(Adapted from *The Lingering Lessons of the EV* by Marybeth Holleman. *Ecologist:* May 2004. p 12)

Which of the following best summarises the main conclusion of the argument?

A The worst aspect of the Exxon Valdez oil spill is that its consequences are not yet played out.

B Despite the research on the coastal ecosystem, the affected environment has not returned to normal.

C Much of the damage caused by the Exxon Valdez oil spill was due to the particular nature of the coastal line.

D The harmful effects of the oil are greater now than they were when the Exxon Valdez spilled its cargo.

E There will be oil on Alaska's beaches decades from now.

15 This is another straightforward exercise in argument analysis and comprehension: identifying the conclusion and matching it with the statement that most accurately summarises it.

Like many arguments this one begins with its conclusion and then gives reasons in the form of evidence to support it. The evidence is as follows:

1. Despite intense research the 10,000 square mile area is far from recovered

2. There are lingering and unanticipated injuries

3. 100 tons of toxic oil remains on beaches

4. The oil is even more toxic than when it spilled

5. It will remain for decades

We also know that the oil spill was in 1989 and the article is dated 2004. From this, and especially from 4 and 5, it is concluded that the worst of what ensued from the Exxon Valdez oil spill is that it 'isn't yet history'. This is expressed by **A**, though in different words.

To confirm that you have chosen the best option, you need to eliminate each of **B** to **E**.

B is part of the evidence, item 1 in the list above.

C is not stated at all in the passage. It could be an explanation for some of the facts, but you would have to have information beyond the passage to know that.

D is the main premise—item 4 in the list. It is the one that allows the author to say that the worst aspect of the disaster is that it is still going on.

E is further evidence, namely item 5 in the list.

16 It is predicted that battery capacity for the next generation of mobile phones will have to rise by around 10% a year to power the ever-increasing number and range of features that consumers want and microchip technology makes possible – a phenomenon known as 'feature-creep'. But such a rate of advance on the battery front is unachievable. For one thing batteries will need to be recharged more than once a day to cope with demand and, since they can only be charged a limited number of times before they degrade, that means they will wear out more quickly. Mobile phones use lithium-ion batteries which are the latest and most powerful available, but the fact remains that more power means more ion activity, which in turn means larger batteries. Consumers, meanwhile, want smaller and smaller phones.

If its predictions are correct, which **one** of the following can reliably be inferred from the above passage?

A Consumers will have to accept larger phones as the price of 'feature-creep'.

B Mobile phone technology will soon have gone as far as it can.

C Consumers will not be satisfied with phones that need recharging every few hours.

D Battery technology will determine mobile phone development in the foreseeable future.

E No one can be sure what the next generation of mobile phones will be like.

16 The first thing to notice about this question is that the passage is not a complete argument. It has no conclusion. In effect you are being asked to provide a conclusion.

You are not being asked to infer whatever you like from the passage: only certain inferences are *reliable*. A reliable inference is one that follows from the information given, or is strongly implied by it – just as the conclusion of a sound argument follows from the reasons.

For instance, someone might choose to infer from the passage that mobile phones have developed as far as they are ever going to (as option **B** does) but it would be careless reasoning if they did. **B** would be an unreliable conclusion to draw because it could be false even if everything in the passage is true. We are looking for something that pretty much *has* to be true if everything in the passage is true.

A cannot be inferred simply because it is not the only possible solution. Consumers could accept shorter battery life instead, or fewer features. They do not *have* to accept larger phones. Indeed, we are told that consumers do not want that either, so charging the phone everyday may be a price worth paying for the clever features.

C is much like **A**: it may be correct, but it is not supported by any of the claims in the text, so it is not a reliable inference. Reliable conclusions need to be carefully measured or qualified so that they do not claim too much.

D is the correct answer. The passage predicts that feature-creep will require a 10% increase in battery output and that this is unachievable without some obviously unattractive consequences. It is safe to conclude that for the time being battery technology will be the controlling or determining factor, whichever way phones develop.

D is different from **A**, **B** and **C** in one very important way: what it claims is *weaker*. We use the word 'weaker' here in a special logical sense to mean less assertive, less definite. That is what makes it a safer, more reliable conclusion. It doesn't say that battery technology will *always* be in the driving seat: it qualifies it by saying that it will do so 'in the foreseeable future'. If at some stage a new kind of super-battery is invented, the situation may change; but that is in the *unforeseeable* future, so it does not undermine **D** as a justified conclusion.

Very strong claims need very strong supporting evidence. If your evidence is not as strong as you would like it to be, then you may need to soften your conclusion by phrasing it more cautiously, i.e. making it logically weaker.

E is different again. What it is saying is almost certainly true: we don't know what is around the corner, for mobile phones or anything else. But the truth of **E** does not follow from anything in the passage. If it is true it is independently true. It is not something the passage implies.

Avoid 'jumping to conclusions' on insufficient grounds.

17 The argument for replacing the present electoral system with a form of proportional representation (PR) is self-defeating. Oh yes, in the short term it would gratify those supporters of the losing parties who complain the existing rules are unfair and undemocratic, but it would end the days of strong, single-party rule and be bad for the country. The ultimate purpose of an election is to install a government that can provide decisive and effective legislation. A single party with an overall majority in the House of Commons can press through its manifesto policies without the need for negotiation and horse-trading. PR would almost always result in coalition governments, composed of two or more parties. The electorate may get the proportion of MPs that they voted for, but they won't get a government that can deliver the goods.

Which of the following is an implicit assumption of the above argument?

A It is only the losing parties who favour a change to PR.

B The present electoral system is fair and democratic.

C Strong government is more important than fair elections.

D All PR would do is gratify disaffected voters.

(E) A coalition government cannot legislate decisively and effectively.

You can expect a number of questions in the BMAT that are based on implicit assumptions. But the argument we have seen here might have been approached equally well via a different question.

For example:

Which of the following would, if true, most weaken the argument?

X In many countries coalition governments legislate extremely effectively.

Y Some supporters of the government would support a change to PR.

The correct response, of course, would be **X**, since the very opposite of **X** had to be assumed to prop up the original argument. By challenging the assumption you challenge the argument. So if it is true that in many countries with coalition governments there is no problem passing effective laws, the author's argument is weakened.

There is an important lesson in this: what appear to be quite different critical activities are often more closely related than you might think. Realising and exploiting this interrelation can be of great value in developing your reasoning skills. As you prepare for the BMAT, take some time to look beyond each sample question and ask yourself a range of critical questions:

● What is the *conclusion*?

● What is *assumed*?

● Is there a *flaw*?

● What kinds of further evidence would weaken (or strengthen) the argument?

Looking at arguments from several different angles will make you a better critical thinker.

Each of these questions will help you to answer each of the others, and in the process help you to deepen your understanding of argument. The questions in the test will make more sense to you and the answers will be easier to anticipate, even before you look at the multiple-choice options.

17 The backbone of this argument is as follows. Three main premises (P1 – P3) are offered in support of the first intermediate conclusion (C1), which in turn leads to the main conclusion (C2) stated at the beginning of the argument.

(P1)   The purpose of elections is to install a government that can legislate decisively and effectively

(P2)   A single party … can press through its policies

But …

(P3)   PR would result would result in coalitions

Therefore:

(C1)   The electorate won't get a government that can deliver the goods (under PR)

Therefore:

(C2)   The argument for PR is self-defeating

There are clearly a number of holes, or missing premises, in this argument. In other words there are claims that are not explicitly stated in the text but which are necessary to the argument nonetheless. These are what are meant by *implicit assumptions*.

For instance, take the conclusion (C1) that under PR the electorate will not get a government that can deliver the goods – 'goods' here presumably meaning decisive and effective legislation. But (C1) follows from the three stated premises only if we assume that coalition governments cannot deliver such goods. (P2) implies that single party governments *can*, in the sense that they can push through their policies; but that does not mean coalitions *cannot*. This is what is stated by option **E**, making **E** the correct response.

To look at this another way: if **E** is not assumed, or worse still if **E** is denied, then the argument would fail, because then possibly the electorate *could* have PR *and* decisive, effective legislation; the argument would not be self-defeating. This gives us two ways of identifying implicit assumptions. One is to look for something that is missing from the argument, or necessary to it; the other is to look for something which would upset the argument if it were challenged. **E** meets both these criteria.

Note that being *implied* is not, on its own, enough to make something an assumption. It must, as we have seen, also be necessary to the argument. This is especially so if 'implied' is understood in its loose sense to mean 'suggested', 'hinted at' or 'insinuated'. For example, the author does imply, in this loose sense, that some of the people who press for PR are motivated by sour grapes, having lost an election. (The clues are in the words 'gratify' and 'complain'.) But this is not *strictly* implied, in the sense of following from the premises; nor is it necessary to the argument.

With these considerations in mind, let's look at the other four options:

A does not meet either of the criteria. If you contradicted **A** by asserting that some members of the winning party *would* support a change to PR, this would not damage the reasoning. Whoever supported PR, you could still draw the conclusion that it would result in weak government. Therefore **A** is not necessary to the argument, even if you thought it was insinuated.

B is neither implied by the passage, nor is it necessary to the argument. The author does not even consider whether the present system is fair or democratic; only that it produces strong, effective government. It could be unfair and undemocratic and the conclusion could still follow from the premises.

C would be assuming much more than is necessary. No part of the argument implies that strong government is more important than fair elections. For a start, the author does not concede that the present system is unfair or undemocratic, only that some on the losing side complain that it is.

D, too, assumes too much. The second sentence claims that a change to PR would gratify the losers, but there is no implication that this is *all* it would do. It is much more likely that a change to PR would have a very wide range of effects. But since this argument is only concerned with *one* alleged effect, it is not necessary to assume **D**.

Returning for a moment to **E**, ask yourself: is the assumption, that coalitions cannot legislate effectively and decisively, warranted or not? This opens up another kind of critical thinking question. For if you consider the assumption *un*warranted, you are in effect saying that the argument is weakened, or even flawed.

18 People who work in places where staff are made redundant suffer more ill health than other workers, even if they do not themselves lose their job. Researchers surveyed a cross section of large companies and found that the increase in sickness matched the increase in "downsizing"–a euphemism for getting rid of workers in order to reduce labour costs. Deaths among employees, from all causes, increased by 21% in the five years following minor downsizing; where major job losses had occurred, deaths increased by 100% over the same interval. Clearly, therefore, the fear of suddenly finding themselves out of work has a highly detrimental effect on employees' physical wellbeing.

Which (one or more) of the following, if true, would seriously weaken the above argument?

A After five years the death rate among employees returned to pre-downsizing levels.

B Downsizing invariably increased the workload on the remaining employees.

The increased workload causes illness not fear of losing job.

C The average age of those made redundant was 12.7 years higher than that of the staff who were retained.

D The incidence of death or serious illness did not increase among those who were actually made redundant.

As with the previous example, this passage could have been approached from several different angles, all of which are worth exploring to broaden critical understanding. For example, the question could have been:

Which of the following is an implicit *assumption*?

W That worsened health of the remaining workforce did not have some other cause, such as increased workload.

X That the mortality rate remained high after the five-year period had elapsed.

You will have had no trouble choosing **W** now that you are aware of the weakness in the argument. W has to be assumed for the conclusion to stand; as we have seen, it would be unsafe if there were other alternative explanations. **X** on the other hand does not have to be assumed. The conclusion could stand even if **X** were shown to be false.

Yet another way this question might have been phrased is:

Which (one or more) of the following identifies the *flaw* in the argument?

Y It assumes that fear of job-loss is the only plausible explanation.

Z It ignores the possibility that the effect on employees' health is caused by increased workload.

Again, you should have no trouble in spotting that both **Y** and **Z** expose the flaw, though in slightly different ways. However, you might not have been so confident about this if you had not explored the argument and its shortcoming so thoroughly.

18 This argument is poor. The conclusion that it draws in the last sentence is not supported by the evidence, which tells us only of a *correlation* between ill health/higher death rates and downsizing. It does not indicate what the causal explanation for these outcomes is. The author just *assumes* that it is fear of redundancy.

Whilst this might be a perfectly plausible reason for the deterioration in employees' health, it is not the only plausible one. Hence any suggestion that there might be a credible alternative explanation would naturally weaken the argument. Option **B** clearly points to such an alternative, for if the workload increases for the workers remaining after the redundancies, then it would not be surprising if, for example, more stress-related illnesses resulted. **B** would also help to explain why the death rate increased in proportion to the extent of the downsizing. This is not to say that the workload hypothesis is *the* explanation, any more than the fear of redundancy was. The point is that we don't know enough from the research findings to say what the explanation is. It is enough that **B** *could* be the explanation for it to be a serious challenge to the argument.

Because more than one response may be correct, we have to look at the other three options and see if they too could pose a challenge. In fact, none of them do.

A tells us that after five years the alarming death rates had returned to pre-redundancy levels. That would not be surprising: people do tend to stop worrying as time passes. If anything, **A** would strengthen the argument because it would rule out explanations like **B**, since the increased stress would *not* necessarily diminish after five years.

C claims that the redundancies tended to be among the older employers, leaving a younger workforce behind. This has no impact on the argument at all.

D does not weaken the argument either. The conclusion is that it is the *fear* of redundancy that is having the detrimental effect. That actual redundancy might not have such drastic consequences can be explained and accommodated in several ways. For example, it could simply be that many of those who lost their jobs quickly found others, so that their fears were unfounded, or that many took early retirement and their health benefited. **D** and the conclusion could therefore both be true.

> Notice that in a proportion of BMAT questions, this one included, there may be more than one correct response. Where this is the case it will be clearly indicated in the wording of the question.

Correlation v caus

19 At 11 years of age, the children of parents who do not smoke are on average taller than the children of parents who do smoke. It is clear therefore that passive smoking, in this case the inhaling of their parents' smoke, tends to set back the growth rate of young children.

conc = passive smoking ↓ growth rate

Even if the evidence is correct, which **two** of the following show that the conclusion is unsafe?

A It may be the case that, on average, parents who smoke spend a smaller proportion of their income on food than non-smokers.

B It may be the case that by 13 years of age the children of parents who smoke are the same height, on average, as the children of parents who do not smoke.

C It may be the case that many individual 11-year-olds with parents who smoke are significantly taller than many 11-year-olds whose parents have never smoked.

D It may be the case that a genetic tendency to grow more slowly in childhood is linked with a disposition to tobacco addiction.

Questions about flaws and reasoning errors occur regularly in the BMAT, although the exact form in which they are presented can vary. You might be asked to choose a statement or statements that straightforwardly *describe* the flaw, e.g. 'It confuses cause with correlation'. Or you might be asked to identify the flaw more obliquely, as you were in the above question, by picking out the claims that *expose* what is wrong with the argument, or what is unsafe about its conclusion.

Often the fact that an argument is flawed will be very obvious, yet saying what is wrong with it may be much more demanding. Practise finding different ways to describe and/or expose flaws when you suspect an argument contains one. Another good exercise is to make up flawed examples of your own.

19 This question is asking you to select statements that show the argument is flawed, i.e. why the conclusion might not follow from the evidence, even if the evidence is correct.

The fault in the argument is a very common one: the author wrongly infers that just because there is a *correlation* between smoking by parents and below average height in their 11-year-old children, that one is the *cause* of the other. Correlation often is an indication of causal connection, but not here. The author has jumped to a conclusion, making an unwarranted assumption about the link between the two findings. It is unwarranted because (1) there are no independent grounds for making it and (2) if it were put into words – e.g. 'Tobacco smoke retards growth' – it would assume more or less what it aims to conclude.

Another way to describe the flaw is to say that the argument ignores alternative explanations. The effect of passive smoking on the children of parents who smoke seems a reasonable explanation for slower growth, but that does not make it the only possible one. As long as there any other contenders, that makes the conclusion unsafe. They do not even have to be as plausible as the conclusion, so long as they are not absurdly far-fetched. However, the more plausible they are, the stronger their challenge to the argument.

The four options **A** to **D** all begin with the phrase, 'It may be the case that...' indicating that they express *possibilities*. In **A**, it is that parents who smoke may spend less of their money on food than those who don't. This is not at all far-fetched given that smoking is an expensive habit that could significantly diminish the amount of money left from a modest income for ensuring a quality diet. But as well as being a plausible consequence of smoking, **A** is also a plausible explanation for slower growth in young children, given that nutrition and growth are so obviously connected. If **A** were the case, then it would certainly throw doubt on the conclusion of the argument. So **A** is one of the two correct answers.

The other is **D**. Whilst **D** is more speculative or hypothetical, it is by no means in the realms of fantasy. Genetic factors are strongly believed to affect both physical and behavioural characteristics. Therefore it is not impossible that people who are genetically disposed to become smokers may also have a genetic tendency to shorter stature, from childhood onwards. This could account for the correlation without any necessity for smoke itself to affect growth. It could all be inherited. Therefore **D**, too, offers a credible alternative explanation.

Neither **B** nor **C** offer explanations at all. Nor do they identify flaws in the reasoning. Let us suppose, as **B** does, that the height difference levels out by the age of 13. Does that in any way falsify the claim that inhaling parents' smoke up to the age of 11 slows growth in early childhood? No. It has no impact on it at all. It may imply that the slow early growth does not matter in the long run, but the argument is not claiming that it does: only that whilst it lasts it is caused by smoke. **B** may also be taken to suggest that the research is incomplete. But again, that does not challenge the reasoning as far as it goes.

C appears to challenge the argument on the grounds that not all of the target group necessarily follow the trend. Some children of smokers, it claims, may be taller than those of non-smokers. That would show the conclusion to be unsafe if it were a very *strong* conclusion – e.g. if it stated that parental smoking affected the growth rate of all children up to the age of 11. But the conclusion is much more cautious than that, claiming only that there is a *tendency*. There can still be a tendency, even if **C** turned out to be a fact.

20 Under employment law a tribunal hearing a claim of unfair dismissal needs first to consider whether a dismissal can be identified. If the employer's words are clear and unambiguous – 'You're sacked' or 'I am sorry but I am giving you notice', etc. – then they should normally be treated as such. However, if they are ambiguous, or if they have been said in the heat of the moment, the tribunal may look behind the actual words to ensure that what has taken place really is a dismissal. Language which may constitute a dismissal in one industry or situation may not do so in another. Also, it may be possible for words said in the heat of the moment to be withdrawn, although in some cases the mere saying of the words destroys the contractual terms of mutual trust and confidence.

Which of the following can safely be inferred from the above paragraph?

  A Words said in the heat of the moment cannot constitute dismissal under employment law.

  B For dismissal to be identified, words meaning 'You are dismissed' must have been uttered.

  C For dismissal to be identified it is enough that words meaning 'You are dismissed' were uttered.

  D The legal definition of dismissal varies from industry to industry.

  E For an employee to be told that he or she is dismissed is not a sufficient condition for identifying dismissal.

20 This example is similar in form to question 16.

The passage is a series of qualifications that make it clear that even when words are used in their literal sense, they may still not constitute dismissal if e.g. they are said in the heat of the moment or are ambiguous, or dependent on context. This makes it safe to infer that even telling an employee 'You are dismissed' is not a sufficient condition for deciding, legally, that a dismissal has taken place. **E** is therefore a safe inference to draw.

By the same token **C** is not a safe inference, for **C** proposes that just saying words meaning 'You are dismissed' is a sufficient condition.

A is too strong. The fact that it 'may be possible' that words said in the heat of the moment can be withdrawn does not mean that they can never be grounds for identifying dismissal. In fact, even if the words can be withdrawn, the passage does not claim that that means there was no dismissal. To be acceptable it would have to be amended to something like: 'Words said in the heat of the moment *may not always* constitute dismissal ...' That would be a very different matter.

B infers that the uttering of words meaning 'You are dismissed' is a necessary condition. This is wrong, not because the passage implies it is not necessary but because it doesn't address the issue of necessary conditions at all. Nowhere does it answer the question: 'What has to happen, or what has to be said, for a dismissal to have taken place?' Therefore **B** is not supported by the passage and cannot be reliably inferred.

D, like **A**, goes too far. The passage states that the language that constitutes a dismissal varies from industry to industry and situation to situation. For example, 'On your bike!' might mean 'You're dismissed,' in one setting, but mean something quite harmless in another. But that would not prevent the legal definition of 'dismissal' from remaining constant.

The logical concepts at the centre of this question are necessary and sufficient conditions. A necessary condition is one that *has* to be met in order for something else to happen. For instance, it is a necessary condition for winning a three-set tennis match that you win at least one set. You cannot win the match without it. But winning one set is not a sufficient condition, since it is also necessary to win a second set. Winning two *consecutive* sets would be a sufficient condition, though not a necessary one, since you could still win the match even if your opponent took the second set. Winning *any* two sets is both a sufficient and necessary condition. If you do it you win, if you don't you lose. Finally, to complete the picture, playing good tennis would be neither a necessary nor a sufficient condition: you can play badly and still win, or play well and still lose.

Misinterpreting conditions is a very common reasoning error, and one to look out for in questions on flaws as well as questions like this one. If on the basis of the above information you inferred that the utterance 'You're fired' were a sufficient condition for dismissal, your reasoning would be flawed. For, as we have seen, the words can be said and later retracted, or understood differently in certain circumstances.

Prepare yourself for questions about conditions by noting examples in newspapers. When you come across a statement such as 'the EU cannot survive without a new constitution' ask yourself whether it is expressing a sufficient or a necessary condition, both, or neither.

21 Argument:

'Ready meals' should be labelled with <u>government health</u> warnings in the same way that cigarettes are. The warnings don't stop people from smoking, but they do leave them in no doubt that they are taking a <u>risk with their health</u>, or even their lives, and this allows them to make a properly informed choice. Recently there has been a big rise in the number of ready meals being sold by the supermarkets. These meals are quick and easy to use and require no cooking skills but they tend to have high <u>levels of salt</u>, <u>fat and sugar</u> and preservatives in them, all of which have long term health implications. It is <u>not enough</u> to list the ingredients on the package and rely on the customer to know which are potentially harmful.

Statement:

The government has a <u>responsibility</u> to promote public health, though not to dictate to mature adults what they should or shouldn't do to their own bodies.

Which of the following best describes how the short statement relates to the argument?

A   It presents a serious challenge to the argument.

B   It restates the main conclusion of the argument.

C   It misses the point of the argument, neither challenging nor supporting it.

D   It lends qualified support to the argument.

E   It paraphrases one of the argument's main premises.

21 In order to answer this question we need to establish exactly what claims are being made in the passage, and what conclusion is drawn on the strength of these claims. We can then compare the statement with these component claims to see how, if at all, they relate to each other.

With some abbreviation the argument can be unpacked as follows:

Premises/reasons:

(1) The warnings (on cigarette packets) don't stop people from smoking, but do allow them to make an informed choice.

(2) There has been a big rise in the number of ready meals being sold by the supermarkets.

(3) These meals ... tend to have high levels of salt, fat etc., which have health implications.

(4) It is not enough to list the ingredients on the package and rely on the customer to know which are harmful.

Therefore

Conclusion 'Ready meals' should be labelled with government health warnings in the same way that cigarettes are.

This analysis allows us to immediately eliminate **B**. The statement does not restate the conclusion. For a start the conclusion is much more specific than the statement. It makes a recommendation about labelling ready meals; the statement is a claim about what the government's general responsibilities are with regard to health—and what they are not.

Nor does the statement paraphrase any of the premises we have listed. It says more and, again, it is more general than any of the premises. So we can also rule out option **E**.

Does it, as **A** suggests, challenge the argument, introduce something that weakens it or show up a flaw in the reasoning? No, not really. The second part of the statement might seem to take issue with the conclusion, but it is a very poor attempt because it seriously misinterprets the argument. There is no suggestion in the passage that the government should dictate, only that it should give people the opportunity to make an informed choice for themselves, whether about smoking or eating 'ready meals'.

So does it miss the point of the argument altogether, as **C** suggests? Or does it give the argument some support, as **D** suggests? The giveaway word in **D** is 'qualified'. As we noted when considering **A**, the responding statement is in two parts. The first part certainly appears to support the argument by agreeing that the government does have a responsibility to promote health. Providing warnings would be consistent with that. The second part is a proviso that the government should not go too far and dictate to people. But that is precisely what 'qualified support' means. So long as the proviso doesn't contradict the first clause, then the statement on balance can be said to be supportive. Clearly it does *not* contradict it because the argument is simply for a policy of warning and informing, not a policy of dictating what people should do.

D is therefore the correct answer.

> Questions like this are known as 'response assessment'. They are a variation on the standard multiple choice question in that they involve comparing two texts and deciding how one stands, logically, in relation to the other. Although they are less common than ordinary multiple choice questions, you will encounter response assessments in the BMAT.

Questions

22 Before the two world wars there were no weapons of mass destruction on the scale there are today. In particular there were no nuclear weapons. By contrast, after the Second World War and during the so-called Cold War, the possession of ever-more-deadly nuclear armouries by the two major military blocs – NATO and the Soviet Union – created a balance of power, chillingly referred to as 'mutually assured destruction'. The lesson of history is that during that time, since 1945, there has been no third world war. If we are to keep it that way we must, whatever else we do, maintain our stockpiles of deadly nuclear weapons. ⌉ Conc.

Which **(one or more)** of the following is an assumption implicit in the above argument?

A There will be no third world war if the major powers continue to maintain strong nuclear arsenals. Conclusion

B NATO would have annihilated the Soviet Union (and vice versa) if a third world war had started.

C The threat of mutual destruction prevented aggression between NATO and the Soviet Union during the Cold War.

D The two world wars started at least partly because there were no weapons deadly enough to deter the opposing nations from attacking one another.

Answers

22 This is a 'classic' argument: part of the case for maintaining a nuclear deterrent as a peace-preserving policy. It has also been challenged as flawed, by supporters of disarmament, who argue that the threat of mutually assured destruction (or MAD) is neither necessary nor sufficient to prevent a war that would be catastrophic.

That makes this a real test of critical assessment. Whichever side of the nuclear debate you are on, and however strongly you feel about it, your task is to look dispassionately at the argument itself and simply determine (1) what its *explicit* reasoning is, and (2) what else is *assumed* by it. You must not be swayed or distracted by your own views on the issue.

We'll start by identifying the main conclusion. You should have no trouble locating this in the last sentence: the recommendation that whatever else we do we *must* keep our nuclear weapons. (It is not clear who 'we' refers to, but it doesn't affect the analysis.)

The reasons offered to support this conclusion are as follows:

(R1) Before the two world wars there were … no nuclear weapons.

But

(R2) During the Cold War… there was the threat of 'mutually assured destruction'.

(R3) During that time there has been no third world war.

But with a little thought we can see that the conclusion does not follow from these three premises alone. There has to be a further assumption that nuclear weapons were the causal explanation for Cold War non-aggression. The fact that the possession of nuclear weapons *coincided* with a period of non-aggression is not enough. There may have been all kinds of other reasons – economic constraints, good diplomacy, lack of appetite for any more conflict, etc. – to explain why there was no third world war. It might even have been despite nuclear weapons, not because of them. If so, then there is clearly no 'must' about it: the Cold War stand-off in the past does not, as concluded, necessitate the maintenance of a nuclear deterrent in the future.

C is therefore one correct answer.

To assume **A** would be to misunderstand the conclusion. The conclusion claims that 'whatever else we do' we must have the nuclear threat. This does not imply that the nuclear threat on its own would guarantee non-aggression in the future. The author is wise enough to stop short of saying that. In other words the maintenance of nuclear stockpiles is claimed to be a necessary condition, but not a sufficient one.

B may be a fairly safe assumption, but not one that the argument depends on, so it is not required either. The argument is that NATO allegedly *could* have annihilated the Soviet Union (and vice versa), and that the possibility of this was there throughout the Cold War. There is no need to assume that either side really would have done so.

D, as much as **A**, is an assumption that underlies the reasoning. The author uses the contrast between the two world wars which did break out, and the third which did not, as reasons for the need to maintain nuclear weapons. If the first two wars would have been fought even if there had been a comparable deterrent, then the conclusion would not be supported. Hence the need for the additional assumption that *at least part* of the cause of the two world wars was that there was *no* comparable threat.

Notice that in this type of question you are not asked to *judge* the argument, only to identify the assumptions. By saying that the argument makes certain assumptions you are not necessarily saying that the reasoning is flawed. It would amount to a flaw only if the assumption(s) are clearly unwarranted. Here it is debatable whether the nuclear deterrent claim is warranted or not, which is partly why there has always been so much dispute over the question of nuclear disarmament.

Recognising assumptions is part of the business of evaluating argument, which in turn is part of coming to informed and well-reasoned conclusions of your own. But for now you have successfully done what was asked if you selected **C** and **D** from the four options.

23 Assuming that everyone has either a high level or a low level of a certain factor 'F' in their blood, which **two** of these statements are equivalent?

(A) Every patient with cancer has a low level of factor F in their blood.

B Every patient who is free of cancer has a high level of factor F in their blood.

C Every patient who has a high level of factor F in their blood has cancer.

(D) Every patient with a high level of factor F in their blood is free of cancer.

23 What is essential is to understand what is meant by 'equivalent'. Two statements are equivalent if the same conditions are required to make them both true – in this case the same relationship between the level of F and the presence or absence of cancer.

Option **A** states that every patient with cancer has a low level of F. This means that any patient with a *high* level of F will *not* have cancer (given that all patients either have a low or a high F-level). That is also what option **D** asserts, making **A** and **D** equivalent.

Another way of expressing this equivalence is to say that **D** follows logically from **A** (or is entailed by **A**) *and*, conversely, that **A** follows from **D**. Unless this two-way relationship applies, the statements are not equivalent. **B** for instance does not follow from **A**. The fact that (**A**) all patients with cancer have a low F-level does not mean that (**B**) those who are cancer-free have the opposite – i.e. a high level. That would be like saying that because all Germans are Europeans, all *non*-Germans are *non*-Europeans. More obviously **C** does not follow from either **A** or **B**. In fact **C** is the odd one out of the four in that it claims a correlation between a *high* F-level and cancer. Therefore **A** and **D** are the only two statements which fully concur.

One rather different approach to questions of this type is to set the statements out visually, or diagrammatically.

Here we have two factors – cancer and F-levels – which between them give us four permutations. This makes a basic Carroll diagram the natural choice. If you are not familiar with Carroll diagrams (or have forgotten them) they are very simple and self-explanatory. You can set one up like this:

How do you use this visual tool to represent statements that begin with 'all' or 'every', as statements **A–D** do? One way is to shade out, or write ZERO, in any box that has no members.

This is a purely logical question. It is not necessary to have any acquaintance with *formal* logic to answer it, though if you do it may be a useful tool.

Some students find visual representation really helpful, others find it more confusing. If you practise this approach you will become experienced at deciding which kind of visual representation to use for which question e.g. Venn, Carroll, flow chart, decision tree, or variations of these

As before, start with **A**. According to **A**, all patients with cancer have a low F-level, so no 'High F' patient has cancer. So shade the area that corresponds to Ca and High F.

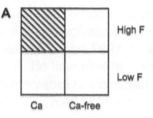

Now you can see why **A** and **D** are equivalent and why the others are different. For **D** states that all High F patients are cancer free, meaning, again, that no High F patient has cancer. We get an equivalent diagram, showing that **D** is equivalent to **A**:

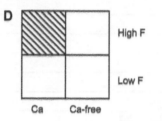

Not so **B**, which says that every Ca-free has a High F and that therefore no Ca-free patient has Low F. Nor **C**, which says that all High Fs have cancer and therefore no High F is cancer-free.

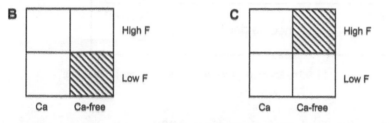

With practise you can sketch diagrams like these very quickly, and even learn to visualise them. Just try making up sentences which express relationships like these and translating them into diagrams. It will help you to grasp the underlying logic of such claims and give you greater confidence and security when it comes to the test.

Skill: Data Analysis and Inference

Questions 24 to 28 refer to the following information:

The Institute for Fiscal Studies (IFS) has totalled up the effects of the six UK budgets prior to April 2003. Its calculations suggest that tax and benefit measures introduced since 1997 have resulted in the redistribution of income from the better off to less well off. A lone parent, for example, is on average £24 better off in today's money as a result of the Government's measures – an 11% gain.

Chart 1

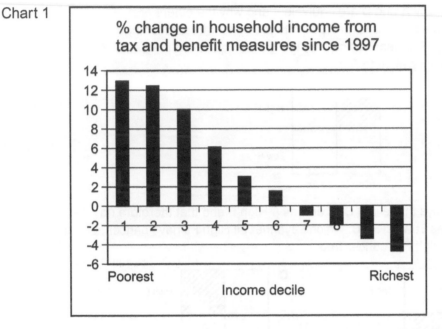

© The Economist Newspaper Limited, London (5 April 2003)

Chart 2 shows trends in the 'Gini coefficient' since 1982.

Chart 2

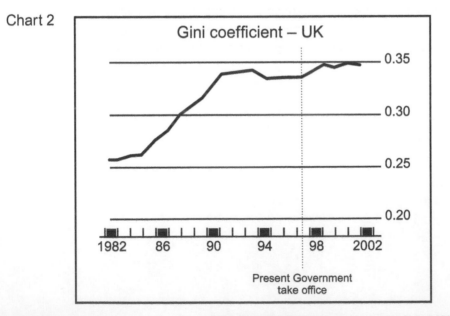

© The Economist Newspaper Limited, London (5 April 2003)

The Gini coefficient is a number between zero and one that measures the degree of inequality in the distribution of income in a given society. The coefficient would register zero inequality for a society in which each member received exactly the same income and it would register a coefficient of 1.0 if one member got all the income and the rest got nothing. In practice, coefficient values range from around 0.2 for, e.g., the Slovak and Czech republics and Poland, to around 0.6 for places like Mexico, Guatemala, Honduras and Panama where powerful elites dominate the economy. The coefficient is particularly useful to show trends. It reveals the change towards greater equality in Cuba from 1953 to 1986 (0.55 to 0.22) and the growth of inequality in the USA in the last three decades when the Gini went from 0.35 in the 1970s to 0.40 in the 1990s (and still rising).

Assuming that the information and coefficient above are valid:

24 Which **one** of the following can be reliably concluded from the information given above?

  A The top 40% of earners in the UK are less well off than they were in 1997.

  B Low earners in the UK are no better off than they were in 1997.

  C Despite the Government's tax and benefit measures, income inequality in the UK has not been reduced.

  D The Government's tax and benefit measures have resulted in a rise in the overall standard of living in the UK.

  E People in the top income decile have seen their real wealth fall by over 4%.

25 Which **one** of the following can be reliably concluded from the information given above?

  A The government's fiscal policy since 1997 has caused inequality to rise in the UK to its highest level in 20 years.   *correlation*

  B Raising taxes on wealth, and increasing benefits for the low-paid, are not effective ways to reduce income differentials.

  C Lower income groups were better off, in real terms, under the previous government.

  D Even after tax, above average incomes in the UK have continued to rise more rapidly than those that are below the average.

  E If reducing poverty was the present government's objective, figures show that they have failed so far.

26 Which of the following claims are compatible with the figures and trends given above?

1 Many of the new benefits are means-tested and complicated, with the result that £4.5 billion-worth are going unclaimed. ↑Gini
2 According to the Inland Revenue, the number of people paying top-rate income tax rose from 2.1 million to 3.2 million. ↑Gini
3 Since 1996-97 there has been a surge in the number of high earners. ↑Gini

↑

A 1 only

B 2 only

C 1 and 2 only

D 2 and 3 only

(E) 1, 2 and 3

27 If countries were listed in order of the current degree of inequality between their rich and poor, with the lowest first, which **one** of the following listings would be consistent with the information given above?

A Poland, UK, Panama, USA

B Panama, USA, UK, Poland   poland Uk usA Panama

(C) Poland, UK, USA, Panama

D Poland, Panama, UK, USA

28 The richest 10% have increased their income after tax and benefits more than the poorest 10% during the tenure of the present government.

If the average gross income of the lowest 10% is unchanged, by at least how much must the gross incomes of the top 10% have changed?

A 3%   **B** 4%   **C** 12%   **D** 16%   **E** 36%

average = x
x̄   12% x increase   4% decrease

12 + 4
= 16

Answers and discussion

Data analysis and inference questions do not require any additional skills to the individual questions already covered. The difference is that the data is more complex and may be presented in more than one form. Data may be verbal, tabular, graphical or a mixture of these. A number of questions ask you to select and apply this data in various ways. This tests your ability to extract, combine, analyse and draw conclusions from the data presented.

The questions above contain information in verbal and graphical form and test elements of both Problem Solving and Understanding Argument skill areas.

In these questions, there are two important things we should understand. From Chart 1 it can be seen that the government has reduced tax and/or increased benefits to the less well off, whilst doing the opposite to the better off. We must also understand the Gini coefficient. We are told that a value of 0 means total equality and 1 means total inequality. The Gini coefficient has risen over the time periods shown, which means inequality in the country has increased. There is an apparent conflict between these two measures. We should also take care with the time period on the charts. Chart 1 applies only from 1997 to 2003, whilst Chart 2 covers 20 years, which is a period much longer than that for which the present government has been responsible.

> As a large amount of information is presented, read through it all carefully and make sure you understand it before you start answering the questions. This will help you to know where to go for the pieces of data you need to answer each question.

24 This requires you to select a conclusion that can be reliably drawn from the data given and reject those which are either invalid or not supported by the data. These need to be examined in turn:

A The top 40% of earners in the UK are less well off than they were in 1997.

Chart 1 shows only the effects of tax and benefit changes on the better and worse off. It does not say anything about either their overall income or expenditure. If, despite the tax changes, the incomes of the rich have risen, they may actually be better off. In fact the trend of the Gini coefficient indicates that this is so.

B Low earners in the UK are no better off than they were in 1997.

Chart 1 shows that tax and benefit measures have resulted in an increase in household income for low earners. This implies the opposite to the statement. We must think carefully what the wording of the question means: 'no better off' implies that their real income has not improved in relation to inflation. We know neither what has happened to their real incomes nor to inflation rate so no conclusions can be drawn on whether low earners are actually no better off.

C Despite the Government's tax and benefit measures, income inequality in the UK has not been reduced.

The Gini coefficient is said to represent the degree of inequality in income distribution. Since this is stated as a fact in the information given, we have no reason to question it. The Gini coefficient has increased, so we must conclude that income equality has not been reduced. This statement is a valid conclusion from the data presented.

D The Government's tax and benefit measures have resulted in a rise in the overall standard of living in the UK.

Chart 1 implies that some are better off and some are worse off following the measures taken by the government. The Gini coefficient only shows the relative change between better and worse off. Neither piece of information can say anything about the overall standard of living. We must also check that the verbal information does not cover this. Once again, nothing is said about the overall standard of living, so this conclusion cannot be drawn.

E People in the top income decile have seen their real wealth fall by over 4%.

The key to this statement lies in the words 'real wealth'. Does the information given say anything about 'real wealth'? Only Chart 1 could tell us anything about this as the Gini coefficient gives only relative information. Chart 1 shows the effect tax and benefit measures have had on incomes, so says nothing about real wealth. It is possible that the top earners have increased their pre-tax incomes sufficiently to overcome the tax changes, so this conclusion cannot be drawn.

The answer is **C**.

25 As with question 1, this asks for a conclusion we can reliably draw from the data, so we must treat it in the same way. Looking at the five statements in turn:

A The government's fiscal policy since 1997 has caused inequality to rise in the UK to its highest level in 20 years.

The analysis of this depends on an understanding of the Gini coefficient. Examples are given in the text to show that a high value of the Gini coefficient means more inequality, so inequality has indeed risen as shown by Chart 2. However, this has happened despite government fiscal policy, as Chart 1 shows the poor to be either paying less tax or receiving more benefit. The rise in inequality is due to things other than government fiscal policy, so this cannot be drawn as a conclusion.

B Raising taxes on wealth, and increasing benefits for the low-paid, are not effective ways to reduce income differentials.

The nature of this statement is quite different from anything else we have so far seen in this question. It does not refer directly to the information given but is very general. The real question, therefore, is whether the example of the UK economy enables us to make such a general claim. This should be sufficient for us to reject this answer – it is claiming far too much from little evidence.

C Lower income groups were better off, in real terms, under the previous government.

This statement is claiming something much more factual, a conclusion on which might be drawn from the evidence presented. As in the previous question – the problem here is with the term 'better off'. Chart 1 deals only with tax and benefit; the Gini coefficient deals only with income distribution. Neither can say anything about whether any group in society is 'better off', which relates to their overall income relative to their overall outgoings. This statement cannot be concluded only from the information given.

If you wanted to look more deeply, you could say that these measures might indeed be effective under certain different circumstances (e.g. a wage freeze).

D Even after tax, above average incomes in the UK have continued to rise more rapidly than those that are below the average.

Chart 1 shows us that, for those on below average incomes, tax and benefit changes have provided a net gain. If this is so, the only way the Gini coefficient could have increased is if the before-tax incomes of the rich have risen by more than those of the poor. This can, therefore, be concluded from the information given.

E If reducing poverty was the present government's objective, figures show that they have failed so far.

Poverty is not mentioned at all in either the text or the two charts. All the information could relate to a very wealthy country where there were no poor – just some relatively less rich. This statement cannot be concluded.

The answer is **D**.

26 The multiple choice options in this question are different from most we have seen. We are given three statements, any of which may be true or false. Otherwise this question is similar in nature to the previous two, although this time we are asked only whether the claims are compatible with the information given, not whether they can definitely be concluded from it.

Again, we look at the statements in turn:

1 Many of the new benefits are means-tested and complicated, with the result that £4.5 billion-worth are going unclaimed.

If this were true, the income increase of the poorer members of society due to the government's tax and benefit changes is less than it might have been. This is clearly compatible with the data shown. The only difference if all the benefits were claimed would be that the bars towards the left side of Chart 1 would be larger.

2 According to the Inland Revenue, the number of people paying top-rate income tax rose from 2.1 million to 3.2 million.

We have already seen that one way for the Gini coefficient to increase while the government gives more to the poorer off is for incomes at the top end to increase by more than those at the bottom end. This would mean that more of these higher earners would move into the top tax rate bracket. Furthermore, the introductory paragraph implies that the government may be taxing higher earners more. One way of doing this would be to decrease the threshold at which top-rate tax is paid. On both counts this is compatible with the information given.

3 Since 1996-97 there has been a surge in the number of high earners.

This is also a way for the Gini coefficient to increase while taxes are decreased and benefits increased for the poorer off. The argument is very similar to that for the previous statement.

All three statements are, therefore, compatible with the figures and trends given: **E** is correct.

27 The information we require to answer this is given in the final paragraph. The lowest inequality means the lowest Gini coefficient, so we are looking for an order in which the Gini coefficients increase. The question says we are looking at the current value rather than the historic value.

We know from Chart 2 that the Gini coefficient of the UK is about 0.35. From the text we know the coefficient for Poland is 0.2, Panama is 0.6 and the USA is 0.4. In increasing order they are:

Poland (0.2), UK (0.35), USA (0.4), Panama (0.6)

So **C** is correct.

> We could have approached this question by checking all the four listings given, but this would have taken much longer and would have allowed more room for error.

28 This is a question about selecting and using relevant information.

Over the period in which the present government has been in power, tax and benefit changes have meant that the poorest 10% have increased their effective income by just over 12%. Similarly, the richest 10% have lost over 4% of their income by the same means. If the richest 10% are to have improved their lot compared to the poorest 10%, their income must have risen by over 16%. **D** is correct.

Questions 29 to 32 refer to the following information:

The table on the next page is from the UK National Transport Survey 2002. Individuals were asked to record their journeys for a period of one week, and yearly average distances were estimated.

Average distance travelled by mode of travel: 1975/1976 to 2002

	Miles per person per year					
	1975/ 1976	1985/ 1986	1991/ 1993	1996/ 1998	1999/ 2001	2002
Walk	255	244	212	193	189	190
Bicycle	51	44	39	38	39	33
Private hire bus	150	131	123	103	95	124
Car only–driver	1,849	2,271	2,993	3,319	3,381	3,410
Car only–passenger	1,350	1,525	1,951	1,973	1,973	2,028
Motorcycle/moped	47	51	38	30	29	33
Van/lorry–driver	122	153	192	178	154	218
Van/lorry–passenger	61	75	72	66	57	61
Other private vehicles	16	33	41	35	24	20
Local stage bus	429	297	263	249	245	259
Non-local bus	54	109	105	95	97	58
LT Underground	36	44	48	51	57	62
Surface rail	289	292	311	290	368	373
Taxi/minicab	13	27	40	50	61	55
Other public (air, ferries, light rail etc.)	18	22	46	57	48	56
All modes	**4,740**	**5,317**	**6,473**	**6,728**	**6,815**	**6,981**

The table below shows details of the survey on which the above data is based.

One week survey : numbers of individuals and stages

Sample size:	1975/1976	1985/1986	1991/1993	1996/1998	1999/2001	2002
Individuals	26,495	25,785	25,173	21,980	23,004	16,886
Stages	365,800	582,798	579,693	486,734	492,380	349,227

'Stages' refer to each part of a journey carried out by different means (e.g. a journey may be made up of three stages: walk/train/taxi).

29 How much further per year did the average person travel in a car (either as driver or as passenger) in 2002 as compared with 1999/2001?

A 29 miles

B 55 miles

C 84 miles

D 166 miles

E 2239 miles

30 Which mode of transport has seen the biggest percentage decrease between 1975/6 and 2002?

A walk

B bicycle

C private hire bus

D motorcycle/moped

E local stage bus

31 The average number of miles travelled as a car passenger is less than the number of miles travelled as a driver. Which of the following could result in this statistic? (Tick all that apply.)

A The average number of people in a car is less in 2002 than in 1975/6.

B The average number of people in a car is less than 2.

C There are more cars with one person in them than there are with more than one.

D Cars containing passengers make shorter journeys than those with only a driver.

32 What was the approximate average distance of a single journey stage in 2002? (Give your answer to the nearest 0.5 miles.)

Answers and discussion

29 This question tests the skill of selecting relevant data. You are asked about car travel either as a driver or as a passenger. Since the figures represent the average over all surveyed, you can add the two relevant numbers:

In 1999/2001 these were $3381 + 1973 = 5354$ miles

In 2002 they were $3410 + 2028 = 5438$ miles

The increase is $5438 - 5354 = 84$ miles

The figures represent miles per year, so **C** is correct.

30 You are asked to sort the modes in to order by the amount they have decreased. First you must select those which have shown a decrease. (Remember to look at the correct time period.) You must then calculate the percentage.

Five modes of transport have shown a decrease (approximate percentages shown):

Walk:	$255 - 190$ (25%)
Cycle:	$51 - 33$ (30%)
Private hire bus:	$150 - 124$ (16%)
Motor cycle/moped:	$47 - 33$ (20%)
Local stage bus:	$429 - 259$ (40%)

An approximation is enough as calculators are not allowed in BMAT.

Therefore, local stage bus has shown the biggest percentage decrease. **E** is correct.

31 Here you are asked to infer what possible reasons there could be for the observation that fewer miles are travelled as a passenger than as a driver. This is quite a difficult question as it requires very clear thinking to evaluate the effects that various scenarios have on the averages in the table.

As in the previous Data Analysis and Inference question, we can look at the options in turn.

A The average number of people in a car is less in 2002 than in 1975/6.

This only tells us about the change between 1975/6 and 2002. It cannot tell us anything about the relative numbers of miles travelled by driver and passengers.

B The average number of people in a car is less than 2.

The average distance travelled as a passenger is:

$$\frac{\text{the total passenger miles recorded}}{\text{total number of people in the whole survey (not just passengers)}}.$$

The number of passenger miles can only exceed the number of driver miles if the average number of passengers is more than 1 (a passenger cannot travel without a driver). If the average number of people in a car is less than 2, there is an average of less than one passenger and the average passenger miles must be less than the average driver miles.

C There are more cars with one person in them than there are with more than one.

This also results in the driver miles being more than the passenger miles. The reasoning is similar to that in **B**, although we are now talking about number of journeys rather than miles covered. All else being equal (i.e. no bias towards long journeys for cars with a lot of passengers) this will lead to driver miles being more than passenger miles for similar reasons to **B**.

D Cars containing passengers make shorter journeys than those with only a driver.

This may be regarded as being an alternative to **C**. If the average number of passengers in a car is reasonably uniform for long and short journeys, the total distance covered by passengers will be a lot less than the total distance covered by drivers.

It cannot be guaranteed that this observation will cause passenger miles to be less than driver miles. If, for example, all the journeys with passengers (although short) had a large number of passengers, and a large majority of all car journeys were short, the number of passenger miles could exceed the number of driver miles.

However, all we need to say is that this observation *could* cause the number of driver miles to exceed the number of passenger miles.

B, **C** and **D** could all contribute to this.

32 This question requires you to select the correct pieces of data and use them appropriately – it can be classified as a Data Analysis question. It is also quite difficult and requires careful thinking about what is meant by average for individuals and stages of a journey.

You are asked for the average distance for a single journey stage. Think carefully what is meant by this:

$$\frac{\text{total distance of all journey stages}}{\text{number of recorded stages}}$$

The sample sizes (referring to one week's travel) are recorded in the small extra table below the main table. Check carefully which parts of the table refer to the survey (covering one week) and the summary (expressed as average in a year). You must also be aware that the average miles travelled refers to one individual and that the survey covered a lot of people. So, for example, you could not simply divide the number of miles in the first table by the number of stages in the second.

If you think of one average individual, he/she travels 6981 miles in a year, so must have travelled 6981/52 miles in the surveyed week, which is approximately 130 miles.

In the survey, there were 349,227 stages covered by 16,886 individuals, so the average person must have travelled in 349,227/16,886 stages, which is approximately 20 stages.

So, the average stage length is 130/20 miles or 6.5 miles.

Since calculators are not allowed in BMAT, you must approximate.

Questions 33 to 36 refer to the following information:

In the USA, the number of serious auto accidents is declining. Countrywide, between 1980 and 1993, auto accident fatalities fell from 51,091 to 40,115, and property claims per 100 insured vehicles fell from 4.94 to 4.00, a decrease of 19 per cent. Credit for this remarkable improvement must go to the efforts of federal and state regulators to reduce automobile accidents and increase passenger safely. Laws mandating the wearing of seatbelts, the installation of airbags, a more robust construction of the car body, enhanced vehicle safety standards, better road design, and campaigns against drunk driving have all helped.

Despite these impressive improvements in road safety, however, Americans now make more claims for bodily injury, referred to as BI. Between 1980 and 1993, the number of BI claims per 100 insured vehicles rose 33 per cent to 29.3, and the likelihood of a BI claim being filed in an accident that involved a property damage claim rose 64 per cent in the same time period.

The 'whippies', as the insurance industry calls whiplash claimants, account for this huge increase in BI claims. For the purpose of insurance statistics, whiplash is recorded as "sprains and strains", and since these sprains and strains nearly all involve the neck and the back, it is reasonable to equate them with whiplash. From 1987 to 1992, claims in the US for sprains and strains increased in proportion to other injuries. In 1987, 75 per cent of BI claims were just for sprains and strains, and 45 per cent for "all other injuries". By 1992 sprains and strains had risen to 83 per cent, and all other injuries had fallen to 40 per cent. This trend is no isolated oddity, for similar changes have happened elsewhere. In Japan annual collision deaths peaked at 4900 in 1993 and fell to little over 4200 by 1997, while over the same period the number of whiplash claims rose from 228,000 to 252,000.

(Malleson, A. (2002) *Whiplash and other useful illnesses,*
McGill Queens University Press, p 254)

33 What was the percentage decrease in fatalities from collisions in Japan between 1993 and 1997? Give your answer to the nearest whole number.

34 Which **(one or more)** of the following can reliably be inferred from the evidence in the passage.

   A The safety features in modern cars have increased the danger of some minor injuries.

   B Not all of the claims made to insurance companies are for genuine injuries.

   C Whiplash has had so much publicity it has become a fashionable injury.

   D The increased number of claims for BI does not necessarily mean that driving has become more hazardous.

35 Estimate the number of BI claims per 100 insured vehicles in 1980. Give your answer to the nearest whole number.

36 Which **(one or more)** of the following offer some explanation for the apparent anomaly in the trend for bodily injury claims, especially strains and sprains, as against property damage claims. (Shade **all** that apply.)

   A Doctors are divided in their opinion as to whether or not whiplash is a *bona fide* condition.

   B Many lawyers have introduced a no-win-no-fee service to claimants seeking compensation for personal injury.

   C The severity of strains and sprains is difficult to assess whereas damage to a vehicle is directly observable.

Answers and discussion

33 This is a fairly straightforward data-interpretation question, requiring a simple numerical calculation. The relevant part of the document is the last sentence, which tells us that collision deaths in Japan fell by 700 from 4900 in the period we are concerned with.

So the percentage decrease is $\frac{700}{4900} \times 100\%$. This is 14% to the nearest 1%.

34 The answer is **D** only.

The data in the passage presents us with a discrepancy, or 'oddity' to use the author's own word from paragraph three. The trend in road accidents is downwards, as is the trend in overall insurance claims. Yet one particular category of claim – strains and sprains – has sharply increased. Clearly this calls for some kind of explanation: if there are fewer claims the natural expectation would be that claims of all kinds would be decreasing.

A, **B** and **C** all offer possible, or partial explanations for this 'oddity'. But that does not mean that any one of them is a conclusion that follows reliably from the data. As you have seen elsewhere, it is a common mistake to assume that because a claim would explain something it must be true.

So, as **A** suggests, the safety features which have been added to modern cars, and which may account for the reduction in serious or fatal injuries may also have increased the risk of minor ones. Seat belts, for example, can prevent head injuries but may cause whiplash by restraining the passenger's body but not the head. However, the only reason to suppose this scenario is that it could explain the trend in BI claims. There is no independent support for it; therefore it cannot be reliably inferred.

B and **C** could also explain some of the increase in BI claims. If people have realised that it is quite easy to fake a sprain or strain injury, this might account for a rise in the number of insurance claims. So might the fact, if it is a fact, that whiplash has been talked up into a fashionable injury. But in both cases, offering an explanation is insufficient reason to infer that something is true.

D doesn't claim anything positive or as definite as the other options. The passage does observe that the rise in the number of BI claims is not matched either by more claims in general, or more fatalities. From this it can reliably be inferred that the rise in claims does not indicate that driving is more hazardous. Even if it *is* more hazardous, the data doesn't indicate it. So **D** is a safe, if uninformative, conclusion to draw.

> Note that this type of question does not always amount to looking for a weak or negative claim. Some sources of information can support very strong and assertive conclusions – but not this one.

35 Like the first question, this is a combination of data interpretation and numerical calculation. The middle paragraph tells us that between 1980 and 1993 the number of BI claims per hundred has risen by 33% to 29.3. That means that 133% of 1980 figure is equal to 29.3. Therefore to find the 1980 figure you need to divide 29.3 by $\frac{133}{100}$ (i.e. multiply 29.3 by $\frac{100}{133}$). 2930/133 is 22 to the nearest whole number.

> You should be able to work this out in your head or you can use rough paper.

You may have decided to treat 33% as a third and calculate that one and one third ($\frac{4}{3}$) times the 1980 figure would be 29.3: $\frac{3}{4} \times 29.3 = 87.9 \div 4 = 21.9$, so again you arrive at 22 to the nearest whole number.

If you like to see this algebraically, let x be (100% of) the 1980 figure. The 1997 figure will then be $x + \frac{x}{4}$ (or $x + \frac{33x}{100}$), giving the equation: $\frac{4x}{3} = 29.3$

So: $4x = 29.3 \times 3 = 87.9$

So $x = \frac{87.4}{4} = 21.9$

If you rounded 29.3 to 30 you would have got 22.5. However, since you would already have rounded up (by 0.7), that would suggest that you round the answer down to 22, rather than up to 23. This would be fairly rough approximation to rely on, but on this occasion it would have given you the right answer.

The mistake to avoid is to take a third of 29.3, or 30 if you rounded up, and subtract it. This will give you an answer of approximately 20. It is obvious why this is wrong when you stop to think about it. It is the lower figure that has risen by 33%, not the higher figure that has fallen by 33%.

You can see that this is not just a data-extraction exercise. There are problem-solving elements in it as well: procedures to select, decisions to make, including whether or not you can safely approximate the figures to 30 or $\frac{1}{3}$.

A lot will depend on your own mathematical confidence and familiarity with percentages and fractions. It is GCSE-level mathematics, but if you are a bit rusty it is well worth getting in a bit of practice on simple calculations and problems. For instance: If your part time job pays 3% more than it did a year ago, and is now £5.30 an hour, what was it then? This is structurally the same problem as the one you have just worked on. If you can see the similarity you are more than halfway to the answer.

> It is easy enough to fall into this trap if you are hurrying and/or if it is a while since you have worked with percentages.

36 This question contrasts with question 11. There you were asked for a statement that could be inferred from the data; here you are merely asked for one which offers some explanation for one aspect of the data, namely the different trend in BI claims compared with property damage claims. This opens the door wider. All you have to ask is: would this account for the difference, if it were true?

B, for instance, identifies a reason why more people might have started making BI claims. If they can now claim without risk of incurring legal fees if they lose, this would certainly help to explain why more claims are being made. If this no-win-no-fee condition applies specifically to BI claims, as **B** implies, that would account for the difference.

C is a little more subtle. Suppose someone is considering making a claim after an accident. If there is no visible damage to the property, i.e. the vehicle, then there is no future in claiming. As you would expect, therefore, property-damage claims would not rise, and would fall if car safety and accident prevention have improved (as they evidently have). The same constraint would not apply to someone making a claim for a sprain or strain, because it would not be visible. This may not explain why claims have increased in general but it would offer *some* explanation for the difference – and that is all you were asked for.

A does not offer any explanation at all. If anything, you might expect this to cast doubt on some BI claims and discourage rather than encourage them.

The correct answer to the question is therefore **B** and **C**.

Scientific Knowledge and Applications

Introduction

Section 2 of the BMAT is designed to test whether you have the core knowledge, and the ability to apply that knowledge, that is needed to study biomedical sciences at a high level. In many respects, you will be expected to apply the same skills that are tested in Section 1. However, whereas the questions in Section 1 contain all the information needed to find the solution, questions in Section 2 require you to demonstrate additional knowledge, and to apply that knowledge appropriately to the problems that are presented.

This section of the test contains 27 questions, each worth one mark. These are based on the traditional subject areas as follows:

- Biology (6–8 questions)
- Chemistry (6–8 questions)
- Physics (6–8 questions)
- Mathematics (5–7 questions)

The time allowed for Section 2 is 30 minutes, so you have just over one minute per question. Although you should be able to complete this section in the time allowed, you are advised to work quickly. If you find a particular question difficult or time-consuming, move on and return to the question later if you have time.

Required knowledge

The BMAT specification states that *questions will be restricted to material normally included in non-specialist school science and mathematics courses, as exemplified by the UK national curriculum for Additional Science and Mathematics at Key Stage 4*, which builds on the content of earlier Key Stages. This means that you should be able to answer the questions in Section 2 using only those aspects of science and maths that would normally be taught to UK school students by the age of 16 (GCSE level for those familiar with the UK education system).

The reason for this is essentially one of fairness. The institutions that use the BMAT have different entry requirements, so it cannot be assumed that applicants will have studied any particular subject to a more advanced level than would normally be reached by the end of compulsory schooling.

So the best advice is: know your GCSE level science and maths inside-out. In particular, don't just cram your head with isolated fragments of knowledge, but consider the underlying principles that link all this together, and practice applying your knowledge to the problems found in this book, in GCSE textbooks, and in life.

If you have not been through the UK school system, or have not studied Additional Science and Higher Mathematics to GCSE-level, then a good starting point would be to visit the UK national curriculum website and look at what is covered up to the end of Key Stage 4. The next step is to get hold of some general GCSE text books in Additional Science and Mathematics, and try to identify whether there are any gaps in your knowledge that might be helped by a little study or revision. (By 'general' we mean textbooks that aren't intended to accompany a *specific* GCSE syllabus, which might exclude certain areas of the curriculum.)

Although Section 2 is based on GCSE-level knowledge, questions may be presented in novel contexts, or combine elements of science or mathematics in unfamiliar ways. You may have to reflect on which aspects of your understanding of science and maths can be used to reach a solution. Try not to be put off by questions in unfamiliar contexts. Instead, consider which aspects of your knowledge could be applied to the problem.

1 All endocrine glands can secrete:

    A Antibodies

    B Enzymes

    C Hormones

    D Antibodies and enzymes

    E Antibodies and hormones

    F Antibodies and enzymes and hormones

2 When resting, the inside of a nerve cell contains more chloride ions than sodium ions and so is negatively charged. When the cell fires, sodium ions, but not potassium ions, enter the cell through a channel and the voltage becomes positive.

    What feature of the chemistry of sodium and potassium could explain why sodium ions and not potassium ions enter the cell during firing?

    A The chlorides have different solubilities.

    B The ions have different colours.

    C The metals have different reactivity.

    D The ions have different masses.

    E The ions have different sizes.

3 Below are three statements about waves.

    1 Microwaves are used to carry digital signals along optical fibres.

    2 Radio waves are diffracted over hills.

    3 Ultraviolet waves are used to communicate via satellites.

    Which statement(s) is/are true?

    A 1 only

    B 2 only

    C 3 only

    D 1 & 2

    E 1 & 3

    F 2 & 3

    G 1, 2 & 3

    H none of the above

1   Endocrine glands secrete hormones, which are either protein or steroid molecules. They do not secret enzymes or antibodies. There are some glands which secrete enzymes, for example the pancreas, but these are exocrine glands, not endocrine glands. Antibodies are produced by specialised blood cells in response to the presence of antigens. So only answer **C** can be correct.

> Some questions are quite straightforward and the key is not to look for difficulties that are not there. This question is a good example.

2   Although an unusual context, the chemistry here is quite straightforward. The solubilities of the two chlorides are similar, but solubility is not the issue. The colour of the ions is irrelevant. The reactivity of the two metals is quite similar, as are their masses. Potassium ions are much larger than sodium ions and will not fit into the ion channels in the cell membrane, so **E** is the correct answer.

3   This question tests your understanding of the properties and uses of some waves. It also illustrates a style of question which tests your ability to analyse information and make decisions.

Taking each of the statements in turn:

1. Microwaves have wavelengths that can be measured in centimetres. They are used for transmitting information from one place to another because microwave energy can penetrate haze, light rain and snow, clouds, and smoke. They are not transmitted along optical fibres.

2. Long- and short-wave radio is transmitted using waves with a wavelength of around 1km. This means they can diffract around objects including hills and buildings.

3. Ultraviolet waves have extremely short wavelengths, close to those of light. They are not suitable for satellite communication purposes as they are easily absorbed by the ozone layer in the atmosphere.

So only statement 2 is true, so the correct answer is **B**.

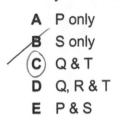

4 The diagram below shows the graphs of the functions

$y = x^2$ and $y = 2x + 3$

Note that the axes do not divide the labelled regions.

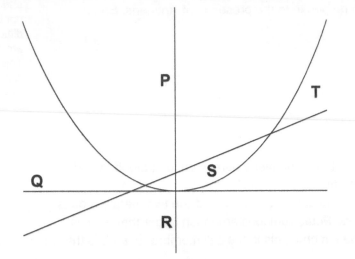

In which region(s) of the diagram are both of the following inequalities satisfied?

$y < x^2$ and $y > 2x + 3$

A P only

B S only

C Q & T

D Q, R & T

E P & S

---

5 The four statements below are about evolution.
Which of the statements are correct?

1 All variation is inherited.

2 Better adapted individuals tend to survive and reproduce.

3 Individuals of a species have variation caused by their alleles.

4 New species develop from variants that are better adapted to the environment.

A 2 & 3

B 3 & 4

C 1, 2 & 4

D 2, 3 & 4

E all of the above

4   We know that the equation of a straight line has the form $y = mx + c$, so the equation $y = 2x + 3$ must correspond to the straight line on the diagram, and the equation $y = x^2$ must therefore correspond to the curved line on the diagram.

The inequality $y > 2x + 3$ tells us that y must be **greater than** $2x + 3$. This is the case in all the regions **above** the straight line, that is, regions Q, P and T.

The inequality $y < x^2$ tells us that y must be **less than** x^2. This is the case in all the regions **below** the curved line, that is, regions Q, R and T.

The only regions where both inequalities are true are regions Q and T.

So the answer is **C**.

5   Variation can be caused by genetic and environmental factors or a combination of the two. However, variation caused by environmental factors is not passed on genetically except in the cases where environmental factors cause mutations that may be inherited. Dyeing your hair or cutting your toenails will not result in these changes being passed on to your offspring. So 1 is not correct.

It is true that better adapted individuals tend to survive and reproduce, so 2 is correct.

It is also true that individuals of a species have variation caused by their alleles, so 3 is correct.

It is true that new species develop from variants that are better adapted to the environment. If the environment changes then those individuals that have adaptations that enable them to survive and breed will pass on their variation to their offspring. Less well adapted individuals are less likely to survive to breed, so their genes are less likely to be passed on, so 4 is also correct.

Statements 2, 3 and 4 form part of Darwin's theory of evolution occurring by the process of natural selection, so the correct answer is **D**.

6 You have the elements: $^{28}_{14}Si$, $^{9}_{5}B$, $^{14}_{7}N$.

Select the answer that has their correct group numbers in the periodic table.

	Group number		
	Silicon	Boron	Nitrogen
A	IV	II	V
B	VI	IV	VII
C	VI	II	VII
D	IV	V	VII
(E)	IV	III	V
F	VI	III	V

7 A security light is connected as shown in the diagram.

The brightness of the bulb can be adjusted by using the variable resistor. When the resistance of the variable resistor is 25 Ω it has a pd (voltage) across it of 50 V.

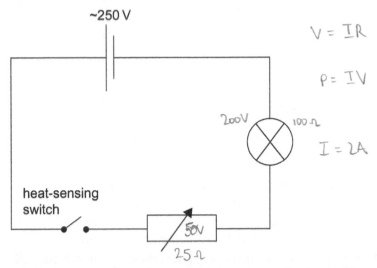

~250 V

V = IR

P = IV

200V 100Ω

I = 2A

heat-sensing switch

50V

25Ω

What is then the resistance of the lamp and the power dissipated by it?

	resistance of lamp (Ω)	power dissipated (W)
A	100	100
(B)	100	400
C	125	100
D	125	400

6 Group numbers refer to the vertical groups of the periodic table and are denoted by roman numerals. Groups are based on the electronic configuration of the atom, specifically the number of electrons in the outer shell. Elements within the same group have the same number of electrons in their outer electron shells. Silicon has four electrons in the outer electron shell and is therefore in Group IV. Boron has three electrons in the outer electron shell and is in Group III. Nitrogen has five electrons in the outer electron shell and is in Group V. The correct answer is **E**.

7 When the resistance of the variable resistor is 25 Ω it has a pd (voltage) across it of 50 V. From this the current flowing in the circuit can be calculated.

The formula $V = IR$ is used.

To calculate the current change the formula is rearranged:

$$I = \frac{V}{R}$$

Substituting the values:

$$I = \frac{50\,V}{25\,\Omega}$$

$$= 2\,A$$

If the voltage across the resistor is 50 V then the voltage across the lamp must be 250 V − 50 V = 200 V.

Knowing that the current is 2 A the resistance of the lamp can be calculated using the rearranged formula

$$R = \frac{V}{I}$$

$$R = \frac{200\,V}{2\,A}$$

$$= 100\,\Omega$$

The power dissipated can be calculated using the formula $P = IV$

$$P = 2\,A \times 200\,V$$

$$= 400\,W$$

So the correct answer is **B**.

Questions

8 Solve the equation

$$4x - \frac{3}{x} = 1$$

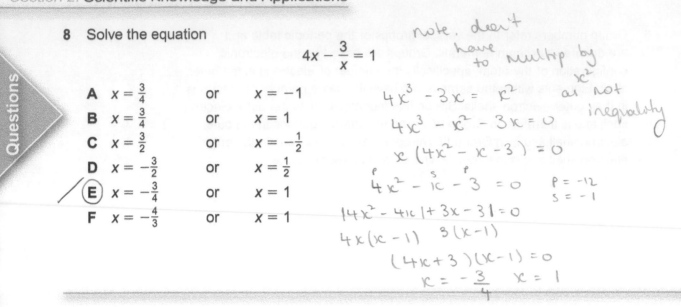

A $x = \frac{3}{4}$ or $x = -1$

B $x = \frac{3}{4}$ or $x = 1$

C $x = \frac{3}{2}$ or $x = -\frac{1}{2}$

D $x = -\frac{3}{2}$ or $x = \frac{1}{2}$

E $x = -\frac{3}{4}$ or $x = 1$

F $x = -\frac{4}{3}$ or $x = 1$

Handwritten working:

note, don't
have
to multip by x^2 as not inequality

$4x^3 - 3x = x^2$

$4x^3 - x^2 - 3x = 0$

$x(4x^2 - x - 3) = 0$

$4x^2 - x - 3 = 0$ $P = -12$ $S = -1$

$|4x^2 - 4x| + 3x - 3| = 0$

$4x(x-1)$ $3(x-1)$

$(4x+3)(x-1) = 0$

$x = -\frac{3}{4}$ $x = 1$

9 The Petri dish below shows the effect of three antibiotics (P, Q and R) on one species of bacterium.

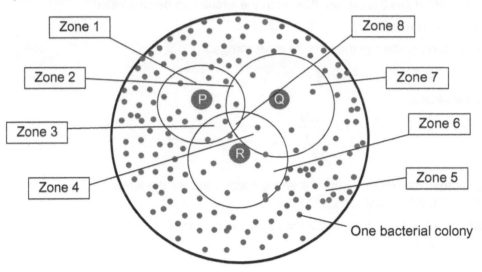

One bacterial colony

Which combination of zones gives the best supporting evidence that this bacterium is developing multiple-antibiotic resistance?

	\multicolumn{8}{c}{**Zone**}
	1	**2**	**3**	**4**	**5**	**6**	**7**	**8**
A	✓	✓	✓					
B		✓	✓	✓				
C			✓	✓	✓			
D				✓	✓	✓		
E					✓	✓	✓	
F						✓	✓	✓

8   We can turn the equation into a quadratic equation by multiplying each side by x:

$$4x^2 - 3 = x$$

We can now rearrange the equation so that we have zero on the right-hand side:

$$4x^2 - x - 3 = 0$$

The left-hand side factorises to give:

$$(4x + 3)(x - 1) = 0$$

For the left-hand side of the equation to equal zero, either $4x + 3 = 0$ or $x - 1 = 0$

If $4x + 3 = 0$ then $4x = -3$ so $x = -\frac{3}{4}$

If $x - 1 = 0$ then $x = 1$

So the answer is **E**.

9   To answer this question you need to analyse the evidence as presented in the Petri dish. The antibiotics diffuse into the agar on the plate and affect the ability of bacteria to reproduce and make colonies.

There are some bacterial colonies growing near to each of the three antibiotics, showing that these colonies have some resistance to individual antibiotics.

Multiple-antibiotic resistance is shown where bacterial colonies form near to two or more antibiotics.

This is occurring in zones 2, 3 and 4, so these zones provide evidence that this bacterium is developing multiple-antibiotic resistance, so the answer is **B**.

(handwritten top-right)
$'58.82$
9.80
$\overline{68.62}$

10 A compound is made of carbon, hydrogen and oxygen. It contains 58.82% carbon and 9.80% hydrogen and has an M_r value of 102.

What is the molecular formula of the compound?

(A_r: H = 1; C = 12; O = 16)

(handwritten working)

C   H   O
$\dfrac{58.82}{12}$ $\dfrac{9.8}{1}$ $\dfrac{31.38}{16}$

5   10   2

$C_5H_{10}O_2$

60

A $C_4H_6O_3$

B $C_4H_{10}O_3$

C $C_5H_{10}O_2$ *(circled)*

D $C_6H_{14}O$

---

11 In which of the following situations does a car have an unbalanced force acting on it?

1 travelling at constant speed into the wind along a straight, horizontal road

2 travelling at constant speed round a corner

3 travelling at constant speed up a hill

A 1 only

B 2 only

C 1 & 3

D 2 & 3

E 1, 2 & 3

F none of the above *(circled)*

10 The compound contains 58.82% carbon and 9.80% hydrogen and therefore 31.38% oxygen. You are given the relative atomic mass of each element as H=1; C=12; O=16. The relative molecular mass is 102.

58.82% of 102 is 60. The relative atomic mass of carbon is 12, so there must be 5 atoms of carbon in the compound.

9.80% of 102 is 10. The relative atomic mass of hydrogen is 1, so there must be 10 atoms of hydrogen in the compound.

31.38% of 102 is 32. The relative atomic mass of oxygen is 16, so there must be 2 atoms of oxygen in the compound.

The correct answer is **C**.

11 In **situation 1** the car is travelling at constant speed, so the force provided by the engine through the rotating wheels balances the forces of friction and air resistance. The car is travelling in a straight line so there are no sideways forces. The force of gravity pulling downward and the force of the road pushing upward on the car are of equal magnitude and opposite directions. All the forces are **balanced** and there is no acceleration.

In **situation 2** the car is travelling at constant speed, so the force provided by the engine though the rotating wheels balances the forces of friction and air resistance. The force of gravity pulling downward and the force of the road pushing upward on the car are of equal magnitude and opposite directions. The car is travelling around a corner so the car accelerates in response to the one force acting upon it sideways. The force is **unbalanced**.

In **situation 3** the car is travelling at constant speed, so the force provided by the engine though the rotating wheels balances the forces of friction and air resistance. However the car is travelling uphill, so the engine must also provide additional force to balance the force of gravity which acts down the hill to maintain constant speed. The car is travelling in a straight line so there are no sideways forces. So all the forces on the car are **balanced** and there is no acceleration.

The answer is therefore **B**.

This question requires an understanding of balanced and unbalanced forces and their effects. Unbalanced forces cause a change in the velocity of an object and balanced forces produce no change in the velocity of an object.

12 Evaluate $(\sqrt{7} - \sqrt{5})^2 (\sqrt{7} + \sqrt{5})^2$

   A 4

   B 12

   C 24

   D $284 - 48\sqrt{35}$

   E $4 + 48\sqrt{35}$

   F $284 + 48\sqrt{35}$

(handwritten working:)

$(\sqrt{7} - \sqrt{5})(\sqrt{7} - \sqrt{5})(\sqrt{7} + \sqrt{5})(\sqrt{7} + \sqrt{5})$

$(12 - 2\sqrt{5}\sqrt{7})(12 + 2\sqrt{5}\sqrt{7})$

$= 144 + 24\sqrt{5}\sqrt{7} - 24\sqrt{5}\sqrt{7} - (4 \times 5 \times 7)$

$= 144 - 140$

$= 4$

---

13 The diagram shows three generations of a family in which phenylketonuria (PKU) occurs. This is a condition in which the liver cannot metabolise the amino acid phenylalanine.

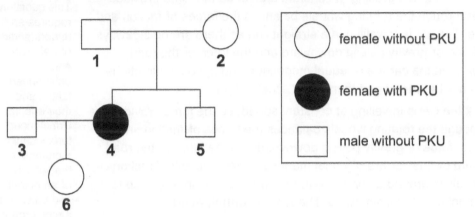

Which individuals of the three generations must be heterozygous for this condition?

   A 1, 2 and 3 only

   B 1, 2 and 5 only

   C 1, 2, 3 and 5 only

   D 1, 2 and 6 only

   E 1, 3 and 5 only

   F 2, 3 and 6 only

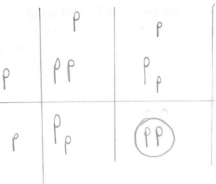

12 We can expand the expression by expanding out the exponents:

$(\sqrt{7} - \sqrt{5})(\sqrt{7} - \sqrt{5})(\sqrt{7} + \sqrt{5})(\sqrt{7} + \sqrt{5})$

which can be written as:

$[(\sqrt{7} + \sqrt{5})(\sqrt{7} - \sqrt{5})]^2$

It can be shown that $(a + b)(a - b) = a^2 - b^2$, therefore $(\sqrt{7} + \sqrt{5})(\sqrt{7} - \sqrt{5})$ = 7 − 5, so our expression becomes $(7 - 5)^2$, which is equal to 4.

So the answer is **A**.

13 Phenylketonuria (PKU) is a genetic condition caused by a mutation in a gene. Where the mutation occurs in both alleles the result is that the person cannot metabolise the amino acid phenylalanine in the liver. If only one of the alleles has the mutation then it has no effect, and the person can metabolise normally.

The key to answering this question is in the relationship between individuals 1, 2 and 4. This indicates that the allele responsible for the condition must be recessive, with person 4 being the homozygous offspring of two heterozygous parents, persons 1 and 2. Heterozygous individuals only carry one allele for the condition, and another dominant allele which does not cause the condition.

Person 4 marries and has a child, person 6. She will pass one of her PKU alleles onto her offspring. The father, person 3, cannot have passed on the PKU allele to person 6 otherwise she would be homozygous for PKU. Person 5 could inherit one PKU allele from one of their parents, or the normal allele from both parents. So both person 3 and person 5 could be heterozygous for the condition, or could be homozygous and not carry the PKU alleles.

The question asks who **must** be heterozygous, so that can only be persons 1, 2 and 6, so the correct answer is **D**.

14 Argon, potassium and calcium have atomic numbers 18, 19 and 20 respectively.

Naturally occurring potassium contains 0.12% of potassium 40, which is radioactive. During the radioactive change, its nucleus captures an inner electron and a proton changes to a neutron.

Which one of the following is formed by this change?

	Element	Mass number
A	Argon	39
B	Argon	40
C	Calcium	39
D	Calcium	40

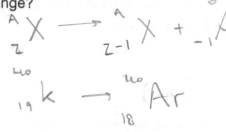

$$^A_Z X \longrightarrow\ ^A_{Z-1} X + ^{\,0}_{-1}\beta$$

$$^{40}_{19} k \longrightarrow\ ^{40}_{18} Ar$$

15 The diagram represents a wave.

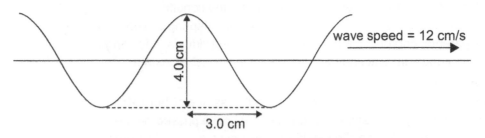

wave speed = 12 cm/s

4.0 cm

3.0 cm

The wave is changed such that the wavelength is doubled.

What is the frequency of the wave before the change and after it?

	frequency before change / Hz	frequency after change / Hz
A	2.0	1.0
B	2.0	2.0
C	2.0	4.0
D	4.0	2.0
E	4.0	4.0
F	4.0	8.0

$$12 = 6 \times f$$
$$f = 2 Hz$$

$$12 = 12 \times f$$
$$f = 1$$

14 During the decay of potassium 40 its nucleus captures an inner electron, and a proton changes to a neutron. So the number of neutrons increases by 1 and the number of protons decreases by 1.

The atomic number is the number of protons found in the nucleus of an atom, so in this case the atomic number decreases by 1. Potassium has an atomic number of 19. The decay changes this to 18, so the new element is argon.

Because there is no net loss or gain of particles from the nucleus, the mass number remains as 40.

The correct answer is **B**.

15 The wave equation states that the velocity of a wave is its frequency times its wavelength.

$$v = f\lambda$$

To calculate frequency we need to rearrange the equation:

$$f = \frac{v}{\lambda}$$

The wavelength of this wave is 6 cm.

So its frequency is

$$\frac{12\,cm/s}{6\,cm} = 2\,Hz$$

When the wavelength is doubled it will be $2 \times 6 = 12\,cm$

Using this value to find the frequency:

$$\frac{12\,cm/s}{12\,cm} = 1\,Hz$$

So the correct answer is **A**.

> Wavelength can be defined as the distance a wave travels during one complete cycle.

16 An isosceles trapezium has two equal sides of length 10 cm.
The parallel sides are 17 cm and 29 cm long.

What is the area of the trapezium in square centimetres?

A 132

B 145

C 184

D 230

E 331.5

F 368

$h^2 = 10^2 - 6^2$

$h^2 = 64$

$h = 8$

17

10   10

h

6   6

29

$A = \frac{1}{2}(a+b)h$

$A = \frac{1}{2}(46) \times 8$

$= \frac{2}{1} 23$

$\frac{8}{184}$

17 The graph shows sweating rates at different running speeds for two athletes. One is running in hot and humid conditions, the other in cool and dry conditions.

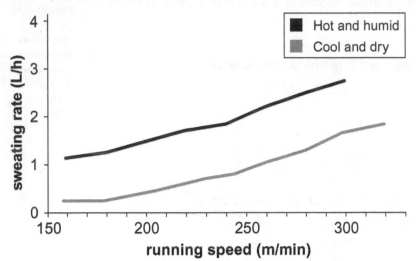

Which of the following correctly explains the reason for the difference in the two curves shown on the graph?

⨯ **A** Vasodilation occurs but high humidity decreases evaporation so cooling is more efficient resulting in more sweating.

B Vasoconstriction occurs but high humidity decreases evaporation so cooling is less efficient resulting in more sweating.

C Vasodilation occurs but high humidity decreases evaporation so cooling is less efficient resulting in more sweating.

⨯ **D** Vasoconstriction occurs but high humidity increases evaporation so cooling is less efficient resulting in more sweating.

16 The area of a trapezium is equal to $\frac{1}{2}(a + b)h$ where a and b are the lengths of the parallel sides, and h is the height.

We know that $a = 17\,\text{cm}$ and $b = 29\,\text{cm}$. We do not know the height of the trapezium, but we know that it is the side of a right-angled triangle with hypotenuse 10 cm and base $\frac{1}{2}(29 - 17) = 6\,\text{cm}$, so using Pythagoras $(a^2 + b^2 = c^2)$ we can calculate that the height is $\sqrt{10^2 - 6^2} = 8\,\text{cm}$.

The area of the trapezium is therefore $\frac{1}{2}(17 + 29) \times 8 = 184\,\text{cm}^2$.

So the answer is **C**.

17 There are two aspects to this question. Firstly, knowing the difference between vasodilation and vasoconstriction, and secondly, understanding the effect of different environmental conditions on the body's ability to maintain optimum body temperature.

As heat is generated by exercising muscles it must be lost through the surface of the skin, otherwise body temperature will start to rise. The arterioles in the skin dilate to allow increased blood flow near the surface of the skin. This is **vasodilation**.

Vasoconstriction occurs when the arterioles constrict, reducing blood flow near to the skin and therefore reducing heat loss. Sweat is released onto the surface of the skin as body temperature increases. As sweat evaporates, it takes energy from the skin, cooling it. This only works effectively in conditions of low humidity. In conditions of high humidity sweat evaporates more slowly, so body temperature rises, so more sweat is released to compensate.

The correct answer is therefore **C**.

18 Copper(II) sulfate produces iodine when it reacts with sodium iodide:

$$2CuSO_4 + 4\,NaI \rightarrow 2CuI + I_2 + 2Na_2SO_4$$

The amount of iodine produced can be found by titration with sodium thiosulfate solution:

$$2Na_2S_2O_3 + I_2 \rightarrow 2NaI + Na_2S_4O_6$$

In an experiment, 20.00 cm³ of 0.50 mol/dm³ sodium thiosulfate solution was needed to react with the iodine produced.

How many moles of copper(II) sulfate were used in the experiment?

✓ **A** 0.01

B 0.02

C 0.04

D 0.08

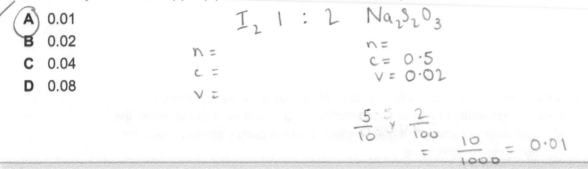

19 The radiation emitted from a particular radioactive source is measured using the following arrangement of apparatus:

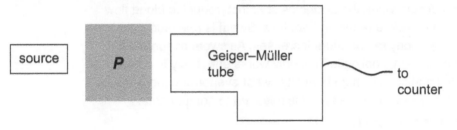

The table below shows the count-rate recorded by the Geiger counter when various different materials are placed in area *P*.

Material in *P*	Count rate (counts per minute)	
Air	540	
1 sheet of paper	540	
Aluminium sheet 5 mm thick	20	no gamma
0.5 cm of lead	20	
2.0 cm of lead	20	

Which type(s) of radiation is/are being emitted by the source?

✗ **A** α only

✓ **B** β only

C γ only

✗ **D** α and γ

E β and γ

18 In order to calculate how many moles of copper(II) sulfate were used in the experiment, it is necessary to calculate how many moles of iodine are produced, which is equal to the amount of iodine that reacts in the titration.

In 1 dm³ (1000 cm³) of the sodium thiosulfate solution used in the titration, there are 0.50 moles of sodium thiosulfate. So in 20 cm³ of the solution there will be:

$\dfrac{20}{1000} \times 0.50 = 0.01$ moles of sodium thiosulfate.

In the titration, two moles of sodium thiosulfate react with each mole of iodine present, so there are: $\dfrac{0.01}{2} = 0.005$ moles of iodine involved in the reaction.

In the reaction between copper(II) sulfate and sodium iodide, two moles of copper(II) sulfate react to produce each mole of iodine, so there would have been:

$2 \times 0.005 = 0.01$ moles of copper(II) sulfate used in the experiment.

So the answer is **A**.

19 The different types of radiation can be classified by their ability to penetrate different materials. α-radiation is stopped by a few centimetres of air and will not penetrate a sheet of paper.

β-radiation will penetrate a sheet of paper but is stopped by a few millimeters of aluminium.

γ-radiation will penetrate several centimetres of lead. It would appear that the type of radiation being emitted by the source is γ-radiation as there is a non-zero count rate when 2 cm of lead is used.

However, it is easy to overlook the effect of background radiation, and this will be detected by the Geiger-Muller Tube. A count rate of 20 is accounted for by background radiation. Looking again at the table, we can see that the radiation is penetrating the paper but is stopped by the aluminium, so the source is emitting β only, making the correct answer **B**.

20 Simplify:

$$\left(\frac{x^2}{4x^2 - 1}\right) \div \left(\frac{1}{x} - \frac{2}{2x + 1}\right)$$

A $\dfrac{x^3}{2x - 1}$

B $\dfrac{x}{2x - 1}$

C $\dfrac{2x - 1}{x^3}$

D $\dfrac{x^3}{2x + 1}$

E $\dfrac{x}{2x + 1}$

F $\dfrac{2x^2 + 1}{4}$

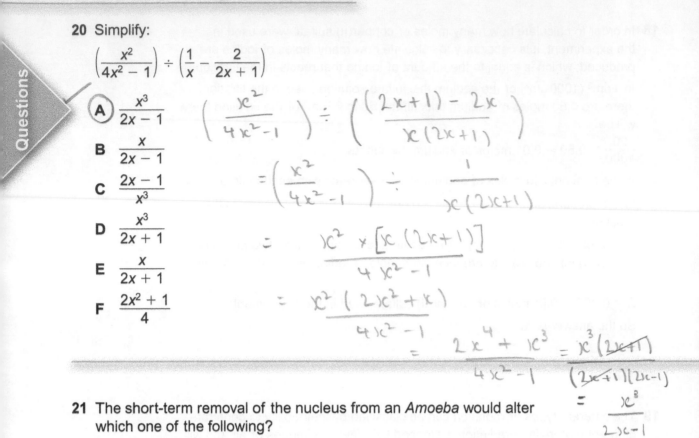

$$\left(\frac{x^2}{4x^2-1}\right) \div \left(\frac{(2x+1) - 2x}{x(2x+1)}\right)$$

$$= \left(\frac{x^2}{4x^2-1}\right) \div \frac{1}{x(2x+1)}$$

$$= \frac{x^2 \times [x(2x+1)]}{4x^2 - 1}$$

$$= \frac{x^2(2x^2 + x)}{4x^2 - 1}$$

$$= \frac{2x^4 + x^3}{4x^2 - 1} = \frac{x^3(2x+1)}{(2x+1)(2x-1)}$$

$$= \frac{x^3}{2x-1}$$

21 The short-term removal of the nucleus from an *Amoeba* would alter which one of the following?

A osmosis (the movement of water across a membrane)

B diffusion (the movement of particles)

C metabolic processes

D volume of cytoplasm

20 We can combine the two terms in the expression $\dfrac{1}{x} - \dfrac{2}{2x + 1}$ by making the denominator the same for both terms:

$$\frac{2x + 1}{x(2x + 1)} - \frac{2x}{x(2x + 1)} = \frac{2x + 1 - 2x}{x(2x + 1)} = \frac{1}{x(2x + 1)}$$

The whole expression now becomes:

$$\left(\frac{x^2}{4x^2 - 1}\right) \div \left(\frac{1}{x(2x + 1)}\right) = \left(\frac{x^2}{4x^2 - 1}\right)x(2x + 1) = \frac{x^3(2x + 1)}{4x^2 - 1}$$

It can be shown that $a^2 - b^2 = (a + b)(a - b)$, therefore $4x^2 - 1$ can be written as $(2x + 1)(2x - 1)$.

The whole expression now becomes:

$$\frac{x^3(2x + 1)}{(2x + 1)(2x - 1)} = \frac{x^3}{2x - 1}$$

So the answer is **A**.

21 The short-term removal of the nucleus from an *Amoeba* would alter the metabolic processes within the cell. The DNA in the nucleus provides the template for protein synthesis. Proteins and enzymes produced by protein synthesis are essential for the metabolic processes in the cell.

The nucleus is not part of the cytoplasm so its removal would not affect the volume of the cytoplasm. Processes such as diffusion and osmosis are purely physical in the way they function and removal of the nucleus would not directly affect them.

The correct answer is therefore **C**.

22 Kaolinite is a fine-grained mineral; when it is ground with water it forms kaolin clay. This clay is used to make pots, which are fired in a kiln.

The equation for the reaction in the kiln is:

$$\textbf{x } Al_2Si_2O_5(OH)_4 \text{ (s)} \rightarrow \textbf{y } Al_6Si_2O_{13} \text{ (s)} + \textbf{z } SiO_2 \text{ (s)} + 6H_2O \text{ (g)}$$

What is the value of **z**?

A 1

B 2

C 3

D 4

E 5

F 6

23 During a game of snooker, the white ball strikes a stationary red ball at a speed of 10 m/s. During this collision the white ball experiences an average force of impact of 50 N backwards from the red ball, and as a result of it the white ball recoils with a speed of 5 m/s.

Which one of the following must be true for the red ball?

A It moves forward at a speed of 2.5 m/s.

B It moves forward at a speed of 5 m/s.

C It moves forward at a speed of 10 m/s.

D It experiences an average forward force of 25 N.

E It experiences an average forward force of 50 N.

F It experiences an average forward force of 100 N.

G It has the same mass as the white ball.

22 This is a balanced equation in a novel context. To balance this we know that 12 H are required on the right-hand side of the equation. To get the correct number of H on the left-hand side then **x** must be 3.

So we will have 6 Al, 6 Si, 27 O and 12 H on the left-hand side. To balance the Al, **y** must be 1.

There are 6 Si on the left. 2 Si are taken up by the $Al_6Si_2O_{13}$, so that leaves 4 Si so **z** must be 4. Therefore the correct answer is **D**.

$$\textbf{x}\ Al_2Si_2O_5(OH)_4\ (s) \rightarrow \textbf{y}\ Al_6Si_2O_{13}\ (s) + \textbf{z}\ SiO_2\ (s) + 6H_2O\ (g)$$

Al:6 Si:6 O:27 H:12 → Al:6 Si:2 O:13 + Si:4 O:8 + H:12 O:6

23 There are two key factors in this collision situation: understanding that when two bodies interact, the forces they exert on each other are equal in size and opposite in direction; and also that a moving object has **momentum.**

We are not told the mass of either ball so cannot calculate the momentum and the resultant change in velocity, which eliminates A, B and C.

We do know that the white ball recoils at a lower speed than the speed it had before impact. This suggests that it has lost momentum, and therefore the red ball has a larger mass, eliminating row G.

The white ball experiences an average force of impact of 50 N backwards from the red ball, so the red ball must experience an equal and opposite force, so the correct answer is **E**.

24 The diagram shows a circle of radius 15 centimetres.

The line AC is a diameter. The chord AB is 18 centimetres long.

The point D lies on the arc AC.

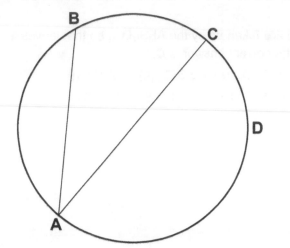

Write down the tangent of angle BDC.

A $\dfrac{3}{5}$

B $\dfrac{3}{4}$

C $\dfrac{4}{5}$

D $\dfrac{5}{4}$

E $\dfrac{4}{3}$

F $\dfrac{5}{3}$

only Cells and organs can be receptors

25 The flow diagram below represents a typical reflex arc:

stimulus → receptor —neuron X→ coordinator —neuron Y→ effector → response

The table below gives some possible examples of receptors, coordinators and effectors as well as the neurons involved. Select the row from the table that represents the above reflex arc.

		receptor	neuron X	coordinator	neuron Y	effector
✗	A	cell	sensory	spinal cord	motor	arm
✗	B	organ	connector	brain	connector	gland
	C	blood	motor	spinal cord	sensory	muscle
	(D)	organ	sensory	brain	motor	muscle
✗	E	pain	connector	spinal cord	connector	bone

24 From rules of circle geometry we know that the angle ABC is a right-angle, and that angle BDC is equal to angle BAC and therefore $\tan(BDC) = \tan(BAC)$

We do not know angle BAC but from trigonometry we know that $\tan(BAC) = BC/AB$.

We know the length of the line AB = 18 cm, but we do not know the length of the line BC. We do, however, know the length of the line CA = 30 cm, so we can calculate the length of the line BC using Pythagoras ($a^2 + b^2 = c^2$):
$BC = \sqrt{30^2 - 18^2} = 6\sqrt{5^2 - 3^2} = 24$ cm.

$$\tan(BDC) = \tan(BAC) = \frac{BC}{AB} = \frac{24}{18} = \frac{4}{3}$$

So the answer is **E**.

25 The first step is to decide which of the items listed in the first column are receptors. Only cells and organs can be receptors, which eliminates rows C and E. The next step is to decide what type of neuron X is. It can only be a sensory neuron, as these connect receptors to coordinators like the brain and spinal cord. This decision eliminates row B. Moving to the third column the decision to be made is whether the brain or the spinal cord is correct. Both of these could be correct. Moving onto to the fourth column again both A and D are correct. So the decision rests with the final column. The response in a reflex arc is carried out by muscle, so the correct answer is **D**.

26 In the molecule:

$$CH_3CHCHCCH$$

how many electrons are needed to join all the carbon and hydrogen atoms together?

(Electronic configurations: H = 1; C = 2,4)

A 13

B 20

C 26

D 30

E 36

F 58

27 The graph shows part of a journey of a train.

On part of this section of track there is a tunnel with a speed limit.

The train slows down just before entering the tunnel and then speeds up as it leaves the tunnel.

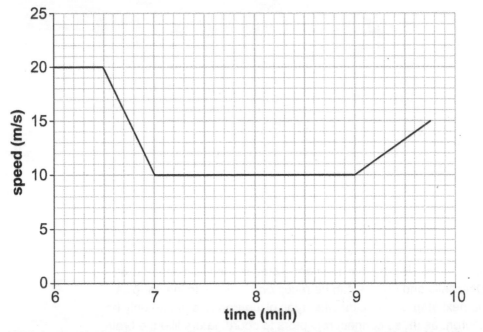

Which row correctly shows the deceleration of the train and the length of the tunnel?

	deceleration / m/s²	length of tunnel / m
A	0.33	20
B	0.33	900
C	0.33	1200
D	0.67	20
E	0.67	900
F	0.67	1200

26 The answer to this question depends upon an understanding of covalent bonding and the sharing of pairs of electrons between atoms. A covalent bond between a hydrogen atom and a carbon atom requires the sharing of one pair of electrons. A covalent bond between two carbon atoms can be the sharing of one pair of electrons (a single bond) or the sharing of two pairs of electrons (a double bond). In the molecule there are five carbon atoms each with four electrons to be shared, and six hydrogen atoms, each with one electron to be shared, giving a total of 26 electrons. The correct answer therefore is **C**.

27 Dealing with the deceleration first:

Acceleration is a measure of how quickly the velocity is changing.

The formula $a = (v - u) \div t$ is used, where v = final velocity and u = initial velocity.

Taking the time from the graph as 30 seconds

$$a = (10 - 20)/30$$
$$= -0.33 \, m/s^2$$

Note the minus sign, which shows us that this is a deceleration.

The length of the tunnel is calculated using the formula $v = d/t$

$$so \ d = vt$$

The length of the tunnel is:

$$d = 10 \, m/s \times 120 \, s$$
$$= 1200 \, m$$

So the correct answer is **C**.

> In questions like this look carefully at the units. The speed is in m/s but the time is in minutes.

Writing Task

Introduction

The purpose of the writing task is to assess a range of communication-related skills and attitudes that underpin both university-level learning and professional work. This section complements the previous two, which have largely concentrated on evaluating analytical and reasoning skills (Section 1) and GCSE-level scientific knowledge (Section 2). It gives you an opportunity to show that you can think about the implications of a given statement and organize a coherent and balanced argument. Because this section tests communication skills rather than factual knowledge or mathematical reasoning, you may find it easier if you are studying an Arts subject. Those studying exclusively science and mathematics post-16 are advised to prepare for this section carefully, using the suggestions below.

The development of the writing task

There have been many attempts over the years to provide a test of extended writing that is both robust (reliable) and useful (valid). The challenge is to give candidates enough scope to express themselves and show the range of their thinking and communication skills, while ensuring that the papers can be marked in a consistent way. A highly structured question format ensures that even the most inexperienced candidates are helped to submit scripts that can be scored, while giving the most able and experienced ones the freedom to develop and communicate complex ideas. The structure of the questions markedly improves the reliability of marking. All scripts are double-marked and if there is a significant discrepancy between the two marks a third independent marker is used. The writing task evaluates distinct skills from those tested in Sections 1 and 2, and provides a good indication of eventual performance in future exams.

Timing

You will be given a choice of four questions. You have 30 minutes to choose and complete your task, and your complete response must be contained on the single page provided for your answer. There is space in the question paper on which to make notes if you wish. The first time you try to follow the suggestions below, it will probably take you the entire 30 minutes just to get to the point where you are ready to begin writing! However, as you practice working through the components in this way, you will gradually learn to organise your ideas quickly. It is recommended that you take around 10 minutes to think through the question before you start writing.

Approaching a typical question

Let's take a look at a typical writing task to see how it addresses the basic skills and attitudes the section is trying to assess. We will look at question 2 from the following Paper 3.

YOU MUST ANSWER ONLY <u>ONE</u> OF THE FOLLOWING QUESTIONS

1   **Progress must always be welcomed.**

Write a unified essay in which you address the following:

Define 'progress' in an objective way. Explain why it could be argued that progress, as you have defined it, might not always be welcomed. Discuss, giving examples, the circumstances that influence whether or not progress should be welcomed.

2   **There is more to healing than the application of scientific knowledge.**

Write a unified essay in which you address the following:

Briefly define 'scientific knowledge'. Explain how it might be argued that medical treatment that is not wholly based on scientific knowledge is worthless. Discuss whether there can be approaches to healing that are valid but not amenable to scientific experiment.

3   **Science is a great and glorious enterprise – the most successful, I argue, that human beings have ever engaged in. To reproach it for its inability to answer all the questions we should like to put to it is no more sensible than to reproach a railway locomotive for not flying or, in general, not performing any other operation for which it was not designed.**

(The Limits of Science, Peter Medawar)

Write a unified essay in which you address the following:

What do you understand by the statement above? Explain why it might be argued that science should be expected to answer all the questions that are put to it. Discuss, giving examples, the extent to which science has limits.

4   **Most veterinary practice in the UK is private and as such it generates profit. This is unethical because the drive to make money will always conflict with animal care.**

Write a unified essay in which you address the following:

Briefly outline what you think the above statement means. Explain why it is unethical for making profit to be the driving force for animal care. Discuss, giving examples, why it might be seen as acceptable to make a profit from animal care.

Read and understand the statement

One of the skills tested by the BMAT is the ability to read formal written English and follow written instructions. The first task is to read the statement or proposition printed in **bold** and understand what it means. Remember that the statement may be controversial and express a view with which you may agree or disagree, or about which you are undecided.

Understand what you are being asked to do

The format of section 3 questions is always very similar, but might vary a little as the proposition demands. The instructions ask you to 'write a unified essay'. This means that your page of writing has to be more than a set of unconnected statements. You need to think about the things you want to say and plan carefully how to lay out your ideas in one coherent argument. The rest of the instructions tell you what you need to include in your essay. There are always three components, and you will always be asked to look at the issue from two points of view.

Remember, we are not interested in what you believe, but in how well you can evaluate the rival claims of two sides of an argument. You will lose marks if you don't include all three components in your answer. You are given four alternative questions from which to choose. You would be well advised to choose one that sparks your interest, but probably not one about which you can only see one side of the argument.

Component one: Briefly define 'scientific knowledge'

You will always be asked to explain either the proposition, a part of it, or its implications. In this case, you have been asked to explain what the phrase 'scientific knowledge' means. Without writing anything on the lined page, but using the question booklet as rough paper, start by thinking about alternative ways of describing or defining 'scientific knowledge'. Question whether a straightforward definition is possible. Think of examples of things that are definitely 'scientific knowledge' and some that are definitely not, and some that are in between. How do you decide whether they are in the 'scientific knowledge' category or in some other category? What other categories of knowledge can there be? You might want to say that scientific knowledge is based on observation, or on experiment, or is disprovable in principle, or can be worked out from first principles, or is about general truths rather than particular things, or is told to us by scientists. You might like to say that other knowledge is intuitive, or based on belief or what other people tell you, or is about individuals. Once you've thought about this, make a note of your definition before moving to the next stage.

Component two: Explain how it might be argued that medical treatment that is not wholly based on scientific knowledge is worthless

Imagine for a moment that you completely agree with the statement in bold. How else might you state it? What other statements might you also make that logically flow from the first statement? In this case, you might add 'Making someone better takes more than a good knowledge of science' or 'Scientific knowledge isn't enough to heal a patient'. What other statements might be consistent with it, but require one to make further assumptions or depend on additional information? Perhaps, in this case 'Science is about general truths, but patients are particular individuals' or 'Sometimes healing involves listening and caring more than scientific medication', and so on. Up to this point you have been examining the meaning of the proposition and its implications, and this is another of the skills assessed by the BMAT. It may be a good idea to make a note of one or two of the ideas that seem interesting on the spare sheets provided.

Next, take a look at the other side of the argument. In this sort of question, you are always asked to propose or comment on a 'counter-proposition'. In the example illustrated here, a counter-proposition is made for you – *medical treatment that is not wholly based on scientific knowledge is worthless* – and you are asked to provide arguments in favour of this new statement. This tests your willingness and ability to examine alternative explanations before you make up your mind. Go through the same exercise in your mind as you did for the main proposition, noting interesting ideas on the rough sheets.

Component three: Discuss whether there can be approaches to healing that are valid but not amenable to scientific experiment

The final task before beginning to write your essay is to examine the relationship between the original proposition and its opponent, in order to identify ways of resolving, reconciling or deciding between them. In this example, you are invited to think of specific cases in which a non-scientific approach might be the most rational. If you have spent your time thinking carefully about the proposition and counter-proposition, as described above, you should now be able to think of such examples quite easily. Think about how you will explain why the particular examples you are choosing illustrate your point.

Writing the essay

Now that you have thought about each of the three components, think about how you will organize your ideas. Unless you are a very experienced writer, you will probably want to stick to the order suggested by the question. Note down the particular points you want to make, and the examples you will use to illustrate them. Because you have thought through all of the component tasks and have organised your thoughts before beginning to write, you should have maximized your chance of satisfying another of the skills assessed by BMAT: *ability to communicate knowledge, understanding, interpretation, inferences, arguments, deductions and predictions by the appropriate use of clear and concise written English*. When everything is clear in your mind, begin writing.

How we mark the answers

We use a team of specially trained examiners to mark this section. As part of their training, they write answers to the same BMAT section 3 questions as you will face, under timed conditions. This means they have experienced first-hand what it's like for BMAT candidates, and will have realistic expectations. During their training, they are instructed in the use of the marking scheme (below) and mark sample scripts. Only when their marking is consistent with the rest of the team are they allowed to mark candidates' scripts for real.

Each essay is marked twice. If the two markers disagree significantly, the answer is marked by a third examiner and a Cambridge Assessment supervisor checks that the appropriate mark has been awarded.

Essays are given a score for quality of content on the scale of 0, 1, 2, 3, 4, 5 and a score for quality of written English on a scale of A, C, E. To arrive at the final score marks from the two examiners are combined; the score for quality of content is reported as an average of the two marks given; and the score for quality of written English is combined to give a single letter (AA = A, AC = B, CC = C, CE = D and EE = E). So, an essay given a 3C by one examiner and 4A by the other will receive a final score of 3.5B.

In arriving at the score for quality of content, examiners ask themselves the following questions:

- Has the candidate addressed the question in the way demanded, i.e. have they:
  - re-phrased the proposition or explained its implications?
  - set out reasonable or plausible counter-propositions?
  - proposed reasonable ways of assessing the competing merits of the propositions or resolved their conflict logically?
- Have they organised their thoughts clearly?
- Have they used their general knowledge and opinions appropriately?

In arriving at the score for quality of written English, examiners ask themselves the following:

- Have they expressed themselves clearly using concise, compelling and correct English?

To help them arrive at an appropriate score, examiners are provided with a set of normative statements that describe the key qualities that might be expected of an essay attracting a particular score.

The normative statements for quality of content are as follows:

Score 1 An answer that has some bearing on the questions but which does not address the question in the way demanded, is incoherent or unfocussed.

Score 2 An answer that addresses most of the components of the question and is arranged in a reasonably logical way. There may be significant elements of confusion in the argument. The candidate may misconstrue certain important aspects of the main proposition or its implications or may provide an unconvincing or weak counter-proposition.

Score 3 A reasonably well-argued answer that addresses ALL aspects of the question, making reasonable use of the material provided and generating a reasonable counter-proposition or argument. The argument is relatively rational.

There may be some weakness in the force of the argument or the coherence of the ideas, or some aspect of the argument may have been overlooked.

Score 4 A good answer with few weaknesses. ALL aspects of the question are addressed, making good use of the material and generating a good counter-proposition or argument. The argument is rational. Ideas are expressed and arranged in a coherent way, with a balanced consideration of the proposition and counter-proposition.

Score 5 An excellent answer with no significant weaknesses. ALL aspects of the question are addressed, making excellent use of the material and generating an excellent counter-proposition or argument. The argument is cogent. Ideas are expressed in a clear and logical way, considering a breadth of relevant points and leading to a compelling synthesis or conclusion.

An answer judged to be irrelevant, trivial, unintelligible or missing should be given a score of **0**.

The normative statements for quality of written English are as follows:

Band A - good use of English

- fluent
- good sentence structure
- good use of vocabulary
- sound use of grammar
- good spelling and punctuation
- few slips or errors.

Band C - reasonably clear use of English

There may be some weakness in the effectiveness of the English.

- reasonably fluent/not difficult to read
- simple/unambiguous sentence structure
- fair range and appropriate use of vocabulary
- acceptable grammar
- reasonable spelling and punctuation
- some slips/errors.

Band E - rather weak use of English

- hesitant fluency/not easy to follow at times
- some flawed sentence structure/paragraphing
- limited range of vocabulary
- faulty grammar
- regular spelling/punctuation errors
- regular and frequent slips or errors.

Where candidates have crossed out sections or added information, the essay should be judged on the quality of the resulting use of English (i.e. crossed out text ignored, and inserted text read as if it were originally in place).

An essay which is judged to be below the level of an **E** will receive an **X**.

Please note that an essay that receives a final score of B or D has been judged to fall between these bands, i.e. an essay scoring a B is judged to be between an A and C and a D is judged to be between a C and E.

Sample answers, scores and comments

The following six sample answers have been composed to illustrate the range of scores awarded to candidates in a recent BMAT. Only Example 6 quotes extensively from one particular candidate's work.

Example 1, Score 0E

> Knowledge can be very hurtful if you can't get better, like your very old or crazy, and its better they don't tell you your sick or anything. If your feeling really stressed and theres bad stuff going down at home having to learn your science knowledge can make you feel like its too much and you need a break from everything. But you need to know lots of facts to be a scientist or a doctor. Its so hard.

Although there are some hints that the candidate is trying to answer the question, they don't seem to have understood it clearly and have produced a few unconnected sentences that don't address any of the tasks set in the question.

Example 2, Score 1E

> It's right that future doctors should be made to see patients at most medical schools from day one. The emphasis started maybe in America, where many people claimed to have been healed by reiki, herbal medicine, spiritual healers, prayer and other forms of "medicine" that are based on belief rather than scientific knowledge. After all, every patient is different and only they know how they feel, and therefore knows how to deal with the problem.
>
> The number of metabolic reactions in the human body that can get wrong, is not always linked to a patient's emotion. Scientific knowledge can always most of the time counter these problems. It would be a terrible thing if a doctor injected someone with a toxin, if it hadn't been researched properly. Not all types of healing can be researched, however, for example psychological healing. I am talking about mental treatment, organising a new lifestyle, these are the so-called alternative healing. There needs to be a balance between psychological treatment and scientific knowledge.
>
> Taking everything into account, not only the scientific knowledge, but the personality and approach to patients what makes a doctor an ideal doctor.

In this answer, the candidate has grasped the idea that they need to talk about experimental science and contrast this with other important aspects of medical treatment. However, the ideas are confused and presented in a fragmentary fashion. They haven't done the first of the three tasks ("define") at all. The sentences seem flawed and confused and the language is simplistic, showing a limited vocabulary. The candidate has not organised the ideas clearly, making the essay hard to follow.

Example 3, Score 2B

Scientific knowledge can be thought of as Biology, Chemistry and Physics: ultimately, the understanding of why everything in this life is the way it is. If we understand this, we can survive and help ourselves to continue to live. That's why medicine is like a science. We can understand what harm is being caused to the body and then predict what effects certain cures will have on the problem.

If it wasn't for scientific knowledge, medical treatments would still be very basic, and imagery and screening devices would be unheard of. In the past, it has been seen that many healing methods came and went, many of them being worthless (e.g. mercury for long life). These trendy treatments can raise the hopes of patients who acquire the healing procedure and when they fail, in many cases is true, then they are disappointed and disheartened.

On the other hand, the doctors of the past did a lot of good for their patients, even though not everything in biochemistry and physiology was understood then. Even now, many traditional remedies, e.g. Chinese herbal medicine, seem to make people better even though we don't know scientifically what is happening.

Overall, scientific knowledge is extremely valuable for giving treatment but it is not always completely necessary. Healing can be given using common sense, without scientific knowledge.

In this answer, the candidate has attempted all three tasks set in the question. It is clear which task the candidate is tackling in each paragraph, and this makes it much easier to read than Example 2. However, the sentences are pretty disconnected and the confusing mix of ideas is made more difficult for the reader to follow by repeated changes of tense (see paragraph 2). This candidate makes one or two quite nice points (especially in paragraph 3) but doesn't resolve the two main ideas in a way that is at all convincing. This sort of candidate could probably achieve a score of 3 with relatively little practice.

Example 4, Score 3A

Scientific knowledge is knowledge that has been gained through scientific experiments or investigations. This means to say that there have been scientists around the globe that have been performing experiments for hundreds of years, usually in the form of testing a hypothesis – if it can be shown to be true on a number of occasions it is usually held as scientific fact. Presently, scientific experiments and research are used to develop and test new medical treatments to confirm their safety and enhance their effectiveness.

It can be argued that medical treatment should be wholly based on scientific knowledge, and that any that is not is worthless. Take for example a "chesty" cough – it has been shown in a controlled experiment that certain drugs can "soothe" the chest and prevent irritations that cause you to cough – this is scientific knowledge. A non-scientific treatment would not have been developed with this knowledge and might not work, so there would be no reason to use it.

In some cases, however, there have been patients treated by non-scientific methods which have indeed worked. For example, there are cases where equally valid forms of treatment cannot be scientifically treated – like the "Patch Adams" laughter is the only cure scenario – we can't put happiness in a test tube and measure it, so we can't prove it doesn't help to cure people. Or using acupuncture to cure back pain. It could be argued that the effect is just psychological, but this could just be because we don't understand the body fully yet. In many such cases, although it may be possible for non-scientific approaches to healing, it will usually be a lot safer to base treatment on scientifically-proven knowledge.

This candidate doesn't find it too difficult to write a page of connected text, and makes a reasonable attempt to tackle each of the three tasks, as instructed. The weaknesses in the answer are largely the thinness of the examples and the weakness of the arguments. The cough mixture example is fairly thin, and the argument that an alternative "might not work" (but it might) is unconvincing. The "Patch Adams" section is very weak, and relies on stock phrases ("can't put happiness in a test tube") that don't convey a sense that the candidate has thought through the issues. (Consider, for a moment, how you might measure "happiness" in a clinical trial, and how you might look for a positive association with "cure". What would be the complications?)

Sample 5, Score 4A

Scientific knowledge is information explaining the things that take place in the physical world, in a way that can be understood and communicated. The theories that make up "scientific knowledge" are supported by available evidence, and may be empirically tested. An example in medicine would be information regarding chemical processes within the body so that drugs can be synthesised to alter these processes and help to cure people.

You could argue that a medical treatment not wholly based on scientific knowledge of this sort would be worth little because it might provide no benefit for the patient. We wouldn't know whether the treatment was worthwhile unless there had been previous practical experiments supporting the use of the treatment. Demanding that treatments are based on "scientific knowledge" is not the same as demanding that we understand how they work, however, as it requires only that they can be proven to work in replicable trials and are therefore useful. The scientific requirement is simply a demand for evidence-based medicine.

On the other hand, there is more to healing than simply curing a physical disease. The caring and compassionate approach of a doctor or nurse can also make a person feel better. It might be that an "alternative" therapy really works to heal people, either through the "placebo" effect on their psychological well-being or through real though unproven pharmaceutical activity.

So, the reasonable course of action is to use the form of treatment for which the best evidence of effectiveness is available, to research the effectiveness of new and alternative therapies, and to treat patients with kindness and care at all times.

This example at first reads rather like Example 4. The candidate can write clearly and the text flows comfortably from argument to argument. However, in this case, there is much more evidence that the candidate has thought carefully about the issues. The definitional paragraph provides a concrete example to illustrate the meaning. The second paragraph clarifies an important issue that might otherwise mislead the reader, and opens the way for a resolution of the issue. The third paragraph succinctly explores a couple of counter examples and provides evidence of an open mind. The fourth paragraph rather neatly sums up the argument in a well-balanced manner.

Sample 6, Score 5A

Scientific knowledge is the understanding of the relationship between cause and effect, gained though empirical study of natural and man-made phenomena. (Empiricism distinguishes "natural philosophy" from "science".) Theories must be tested repeatedly and corroborated by different parties, after which they may be accepted into the current body of scientific knowledge.

One could argue that medical treatment should be wholly based on such "scientific knowledge" as follows.

1. Without proper empirical understanding of cause and effect, we cannot predict the outcome of treatment, and therefore cannot be sure whether our treatment could do harm or good. It may be better not to treat at all.

2. Without scientific reproduction of results, there are no principles that can apply to many patients, therefore treatment must be individual and inefficient.

3. Unless treatment is based on scientific knowledge, it might be incompatible with current medical methods that are themselves scientific and mechanistic.

4. If treatment cannot be supported by scientific knowledge, it is impossible to be accountable for one's actions or to be safe from litigation.

These arguments may not be valid in some cases, but the modern paradigm of "healing" is as much to do with removal of obstacles to mental potential as it is to removing those blocking physical wholeness. "Medical treatment" is really only concerned with the latter. The use of alternative therapies or new ways of working to release psychological potential is concerned largely with the specific conditions of individuals, and cannot be tested empirically, or generalized across the whole affected population. By recognizing this very important aspect of health care, it is perfectly possible for the standard concept of science-based medicine and individualistic and holistic approaches to health care to coexist and complement one another.

There's no such thing as a perfect essay; really good answers can take many forms, and are rarely without some faults. This example, which has only been lightly edited, achieved full marks, even though it could certainly be improved upon. It is much clearer than in Sample 5 that the person writing the piece is in command of the issue in question, has the ability to think about it in an original way and express him or herself compellingly. It was felt that the 'definition' paragraph was clear and forceful, though the 'history of science' lesson wasn't really necessary! The candidate showed greater insight and breadth in the justifications (numbered paragraphs) he or she gave for the 'worthless' proposition, ranging from the purely scientific or practical, to the speculative and socio-legal, than essays receiving a score of 4. He or she clearly showed an understanding of the alternative point of view and made a convincing and practical synthesis of the two in the closing paragraph.

BMAT specification

Purpose of the test

The purpose of the Biomedical Admissions Test is solely to provide a predictive assessment of candidates' potential in an academically demanding undergraduate biomedical degree, and not their fitness to practice medicine or veterinary medicine – which universities will continue to assess in other ways. The test results are intended to be used as a significant component of the selection decision in conjunction with past examination performance, evidence from the UCAS form and performance at interview.

Test items draw upon generic academic skills and basic science knowledge rather than the products of recent specialist teaching, and provide an objective basis for comparing candidates from different backgrounds, including mature applicants and those from different countries. The test is designed to be challenging, in order to discriminate effectively between able applicants for university courses, including those who may have achieved the highest possible grades in school examinations.

Qualities to be assessed

Knowledge

Familiarity with concepts, terms and propositional knowledge specified by the National Curriculum up to and including Key Stage 4 (GCSE-level) Science and Additional Science and mathematics.

Skills

Handling of number and communication, specifically the:

- ability to read formal English and follow written instructions;
- ability to work quickly and accurately;
- ability to perform very simple mental arithmetic;
- ability to identify the straightforward meaning of a particular phrases within a longer text;
- ability to extract the meaning intended by an author where to do so requires more than one syntactical element of the text to be understood and synthesized;
- ability to read simple quantitative data presented numerically or graphically and to understand their straightforward meaning and to be able to produce simple and appropriate graphs or diagrams of quantitative data;
- ability to generalize from quantitative data, for example to interpret a trend, a pattern, a rate and to be able to apply the generalization to the particular or hypothetical;
- ability to make logical inferences or deductions from textual information and quantitative data and to identify illogical inferences;
- ability to communicate knowledge, understanding, interpretation, inferences, arguments, deductions and predictions by the appropriate use of clear and concise written English and diagrams;
- tendency to take approaches that are critical and evidence-based, and which consider alternatives.

Structure of the test

The test has three elements: a 60-minute test of Aptitude and Skills, a 30-minute test of Scientific Knowledge and Applications and a 30-minute Writing Task. The structure of each of these elements is outlined below.

1: Aptitude and Skills	Minutes	Marks available
This element tests generic skills often utilised in undergraduate study. The range of these and the approximate balance between them in terms of the time and number of marks which will be available is outlined below. Questions will be in multiple-choice or short answer form. Calculators may not be used.		
Problem Solving Demands insight to determine how to encode and process numerical information so as to solve problems, using simple numerical and algebraic operations. Problem solving will require the capacity to: • select relevant information • recognise analogous cases • determine and apply appropriate procedures.	30 (approx)	13 3–7 3–7 3–7
Understanding Argument Presents a series of logical arguments and requires respondents to: • identify reasons, assumptions and conclusions • detect flaws • draw conclusions.	15 (approx)	10 2–4 2–4 2–4
Data Analysis and Inference Demands the use of information skills (vocabulary, comprehension, basic descriptive statistics and graphical tools), data interpretation, analysis and scientific inference and deduction to reach appropriate conclusions from information provided in different forms, namely: • verbal • statistical • graphical.	15 (approx)	12 3–5 3–5 3–5
All	60	35

2: Scientific Knowledge and Applications	Minutes	Marks available
This element tests whether candidates have the core knowledge and the capacity to apply it that are a pre-requisite for high-level study in biomedical sciences. Questions will be restricted to material normally included in non-specialist school science and mathematics courses, as exemplified by the UK national curriculum for Science and Additional Science and Mathematics at Key Stage 4. They will however require a level of understanding appropriate for such an able target group. The balance between the subject areas in terms of time and marks available is outlined below. Questions will be in multiple-choice or short answer form. Calculators may not be used.		
Biology	8 (approx)	6–8
Chemistry	8 (approx)	6–8
Physics	8 (approx)	6–8
Mathematics	6 (approx)	5–7
All	30	27

3: Writing Task	Minutes	Marks available
A selection of four tasks will be available, from which one must be chosen. These will include brief questions based on topics of general, medical, scientific or veterinary interest. Questions will provide a short proposition and may require candidates to: • explain or discuss the proposition's implications; • suggest a counter proposition or argument; • suggest a (method for) resolution. The Writing Task provides an opportunity for candidates to demonstrate the capacity to develop ideas and to communicate them effectively in writing. Skills to be assessed include those concerning communication, described above. All specified skills may be assessed. The question paper will brief candidates about the nature and purpose of the Task. They will be required to produce a written communication, without the assistance of a dictionary or automated spelling and grammar checking software. Whilst they may make preliminary notes, the final product is strictly limited to one A4 page, to promote the disciplined selection and organisation of ideas, together with their concise, accurate and effective expression. When scoring responses, consideration will be given to the degree to which candidates have: addressed the question in the way demanded; organised their thoughts clearly; expressed themselves using concise, compelling and correct English; used their general knowledge and opinions appropriately. Admitting institutions will be provided with a copy of the applicant's response. This may be used to stimulate discussion at interview.	30	15

Scoring and reporting

For both Aptitude and Skills (Section 1) and Scientific Knowledge and Applications (Section 2), scores will be reported (to one decimal place) on a 9-point BMAT scale.

The Writing Task will be scored by Cambridge Assessment, and an image supplied to each institution to which the candidate has applied. In addition to scores, the task provides institutions with a basis for qualitative assessments of writing skills as well as a tool for promoting discussion at interview.

Test format

There will be separate question papers for each of Sections 1, 2 and 3.

With the exception of the Writing Task (Section 3), all questions will be in objective or semi-objective formats. Questions or sub-questions will each carry one mark, so that although clusters of sub-questions relating to the same stimulus will be feasible, partial credit items will not be used. For Sections 1 and 2 exhaustive answer keys will be finalised after inspection of the range of responses to each question; followed by automated marking, psychometric analysis, test calibration and the issue of results.

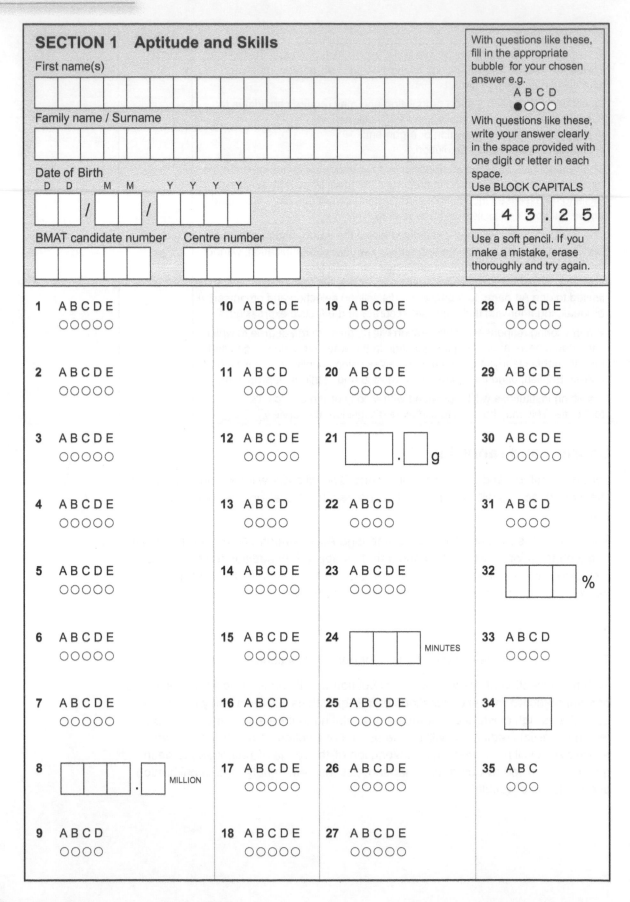

SECTION 1   Aptitude and Skills

First name(s)

Family name / Surname

Date of Birth

D D   M M   Y Y Y Y

/   /

BMAT candidate number   Centre number

With questions like these, fill in the appropriate bubble for your chosen answer e.g.

A B C D
● ○ ○ ○

With questions like these, write your answer clearly in the space provided with one digit or letter in each space.
Use BLOCK CAPITALS

4 3 . 2 5

Use a soft pencil. If you make a mistake, erase thoroughly and try again.

1 A B C D E
   ○ ○ ○ ○ ○

2 A B C D E
   ○ ○ ○ ○ ○

3 A B C D E
   ○ ○ ○ ○ ○

4 A B C D E
   ○ ○ ○ ○ ○

5 A B C D E
   ○ ○ ○ ○ ○

6 A B C D E
   ○ ○ ○ ○ ○

7 A B C D E
   ○ ○ ○ ○ ○

8 [   ][   ][   ] . [   ] MILLION

9 A B C D
   ○ ○ ○ ○

10 A B C D E
    ○ ○ ○ ○ ○

11 A B C D
    ○ ○ ○ ○

12 A B C D E
    ○ ○ ○ ○ ○

13 A B C D
    ○ ○ ○ ○

14 A B C D E
    ○ ○ ○ ○ ○

15 A B C D E
    ○ ○ ○ ○ ○

16 A B C D
    ○ ○ ○ ○

17 A B C D E
    ○ ○ ○ ○ ○

18 A B C D E
    ○ ○ ○ ○ ○

19 A B C D E
    ○ ○ ○ ○ ○

20 A B C D E
    ○ ○ ○ ○ ○

21 [   ][   ] . [   ] g

22 A B C D
    ○ ○ ○ ○

23 A B C D E
    ○ ○ ○ ○ ○

24 [   ][   ][   ] MINUTES

25 A B C D E
    ○ ○ ○ ○ ○

26 A B C D E
    ○ ○ ○ ○ ○

27 A B C D E
    ○ ○ ○ ○ ○

28 A B C D E
    ○ ○ ○ ○ ○

29 A B C D E
    ○ ○ ○ ○ ○

30 A B C D E
    ○ ○ ○ ○ ○

31 A B C D
    ○ ○ ○ ○

32 [   ][   ][   ] %

33 A B C D
    ○ ○ ○ ○

34 [   ][   ]

35 A B C
    ○ ○ ○

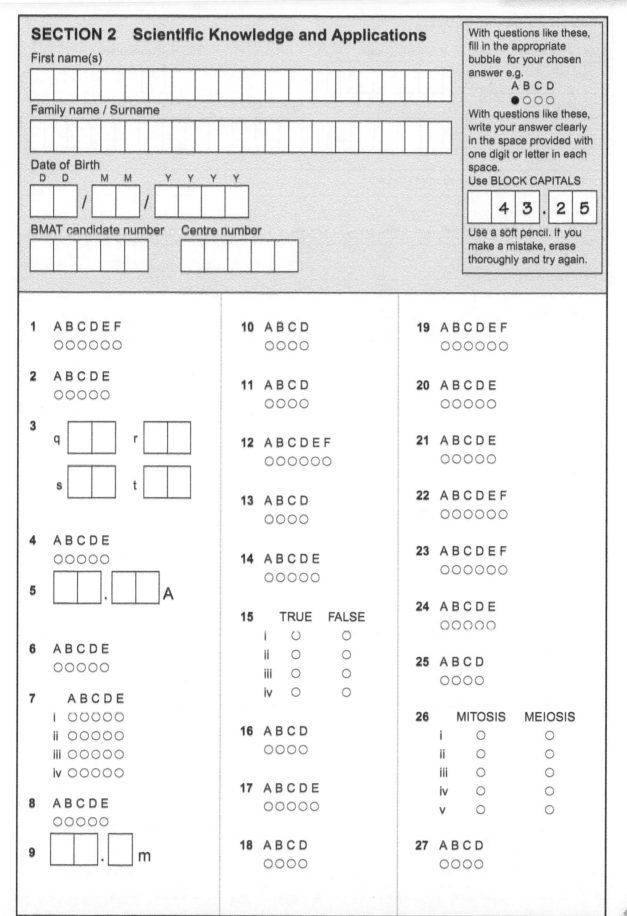

SECTION 2 Scientific Knowledge and Applications

First name(s)

Family name / Surname

Date of Birth

D D   M M   Y Y Y Y

/   /

BMAT candidate number   Centre number

With questions like these, fill in the appropriate bubble for your chosen answer e.g.

A B C D
● ○ ○ ○

With questions like these, write your answer clearly in the space provided with one digit or letter in each space.

Use BLOCK CAPITALS

| | 4 | 3 | . | 2 | 5 |

Use a soft pencil. If you make a mistake, erase thoroughly and try again.

1 A B C D E F
○ ○ ○ ○ ○ ○

2 A B C D E
○ ○ ○ ○ ○

3 q [ ][ ]   r [ ][ ]
   s [ ][ ]   t [ ]

4 A B C D E
○ ○ ○ ○ ○

5 [ ][ ] . [ ][ ] A

6 A B C D E
○ ○ ○ ○ ○

7   A B C D E
i   ○ ○ ○ ○ ○
ii ○ ○ ○ ○ ○
iii ○ ○ ○ ○ ○
iv ○ ○ ○ ○ ○

8 A B C D E
○ ○ ○ ○ ○

9 [ ][ ] . [ ] m

10 A B C D
○ ○ ○ ○

11 A B C D
○ ○ ○ ○

12 A B C D E F
○ ○ ○ ○ ○ ○

13 A B C D
○ ○ ○ ○

14 A B C D E
○ ○ ○ ○ ○

15   TRUE   FALSE
i   ○   ○
ii   ○   ○
iii   ○   ○
iv   ○   ○

16 A B C D
○ ○ ○ ○

17 A B C D E
○ ○ ○ ○ ○

18 A B C D
○ ○ ○ ○

19 A B C D E F
○ ○ ○ ○ ○ ○

20 A B C D E
○ ○ ○ ○ ○

21 A B C D E
○ ○ ○ ○ ○

22 A B C D E F
○ ○ ○ ○ ○ ○

23 A B C D E F
○ ○ ○ ○ ○ ○

24 A B C D E
○ ○ ○ ○ ○

25 A B C D
○ ○ ○ ○

26   MITOSIS   MEIOSIS
i   ○   ○
ii   ○   ○
iii   ○   ○
iv   ○   ○
v   ○   ○

27 A B C D
○ ○ ○ ○

Section 3 answer sheet

BMAT candidate number

Centre number

Question answered

Forename

Surname

Your answer must be contained within this area

Further reading

Aptitude and Skills

Thinking Skills, John Butterworth & Geoff Thwaites,
Cambridge University Press (2005) ISBN: 0521521491

AS Critical Thinking for OCR: Credibility of Evidence, Jacquie Thwaites,
Heinemann (2005) ISBN: 0435235818

AS Critical Thinking for OCR: Assessing and Developing Argument,
Mark McBride, Jo Lally, Dave Wells, Heinemann (2006) ISBN: 0435235842

AS Critical Thinking for OCR: Critical Reasoning, Heinemann (2006)
ISBN: 0435235850

Critical Thinking: A Concise Guide, Gary Kemp & Tracy Bowell, Routledge (2005)
ISBN: 0415343135

Critical Reasoning: A Practical Introduction, Anne Thomson, Routledge (2001)
ISBN: 0415241200

Critical Thinking for Students, Roy van den Brink-Budgen, How To Books (2000)
ISBN: 1857036344

Thinking from A to Z, 2nd Edition, ed. Nigel Warburton, Routledge (2000)
ISBN: 0415222818

Scientific Knowledge and Applications

Any non-exam-board-specific Science and Additional Science GCSE textbooks.

Also useful are the GCSE revision guides produced by Coordination Group
Publications (www.cgpbooks.co.uk) and the BBC Bitesize GCSE revision guides
(www.bbc.co.uk/schools/gcsebitesize).

About the authors

Section 1: Aptitude and Skills

John Butterworth is a senior examiner in Thinking Skills and Critical Thinking, including BMAT Paper 1. He has had a long involvement in the development of these subjects, and has trained teachers in the UK, the Middle East, Malaysia and Singapore. He has a degree in Philosophy from University College London and is an ex-teacher turned freelance writer.

Geoff Thwaites has a Ph.D. in Chemical Engineering from Cambridge University. He worked for some years in industrial research and development and is now self-employed as an examiner, trainer and glass engraver. He has been an examiner in Thinking Skills, specialising in Problem Solving, since 1993. He is currently joint Chief Examiner for BMAT Paper 1.

Section 2: Scientific Knowledge and Applications

Richard Shewry is a professional examiner and consultant. He works on the development of examinations in the UK and other countries, including the BMAT examination. He is also Principal Examiner in GCSE Biology and Chair of Examiners for GCSE Science. He provides continuous professional development for teachers of science to a number of organisations.

Section 3: Writing Task

William James studied Genetics under John Jinks in Birmingham and Microbiology under Joel Mandelstam in Oxford. He has taught preclinical sciences in Oxford since 1984 and is a Tutor at Brasenose College, Oxford. His research into HIV and prion disease is based at the Sir William Dunn School of Pathology. He was the Coordinator for Admissions at the Oxford Medical School for three years and was part of the original BMAT development team.

Cambridge Assessment Editors

Mark Shannon is the Assessment Manager of the team that produces the BMAT, TSA and other University Admissions Tests. He has been responsible for the production of the BMAT and one of its predecessors, the Cambridge Medical and Veterinary Admissions test, since 2001.

Sue Fiander is an Assessment Development Officer in the team that produces the BMAT, TSA and other university admissions tests. She has been involved in the production of the BMAT since 2005.

About Cambridge Assessment

Cambridge Assessment is one of the world's largest assessment agencies, providing a wide range of general academic, English language, vocational and skills-based qualifications and tests in over 150 countries. As a non-teaching, not-for-profit department of the University of Cambridge, we have charitable status.

Our three educational operations work closely together but each provides specialised assessment and awarding services:

- OCR creates, designs and delivers general and vocational qualifications to over 13,000 schools, colleges, employers and training providers in the UK.

- University of Cambridge International Examinations (CIE) is the world's leading provider of international school examinations and international vocational awards, and advises a number of governments on assessment types and processes.

- University of Cambridge ESOL Examinations (Cambridge ESOL) provides exams and tests for learners and teachers of English for speakers of other languages in 135 countries including the UK.